D1320209

real cooking, by george!

anything flambé
requires dexterity

real cooking, by george!

by George Jacobs

illustrations by the author

Parnassus Imprints

ORLEANS, MASSACHUSETTS

Also by George Jacobs

How to Get Along in Portugal and Spain

ISBN 0-940160-32-3

Library of Congress catalogue card number 85-0630

a taste of real cooking, by george!

1   a beginning   1

power eating — you are invited to the author's garden party in albufeira — duck or deformed chicken? — la pyramide by scooter

2   first courses and such   11

the trouble with salad nowadays . . . — crudités taste better than they sound — a brief look at an avocado fertility festival — the lowdown on upscale pâté — super black bean soup

3   seafood   27

fish with a caribbean accent le vrai court-bouillon — the etymology of blaff and is it related to barf? — tips from the cod father acras and gold-plated cod — squid by another name tastes better — with fish that swim through the door — a visit to sardine city

4   meat and garlic   46

eat garlic but don't tell anyone — what to do with a six-pack of thighs — a hot time in the khyber pass — virginia ham lore — lovable liver — hot peppers lengthen your life

5   vegetables and such   66

keeping vegetables green — steaming versus boiling — the great artichoke bonus — what to do with all that zucchini — ratatouille and how to pronounce it as well as make it — the floating potato i.d. test — what rice cooking and martinis have in common — meat a coccotte minute — the 3-minute flan

6   seasonings and spices   92

*16,000 acres of garlic—virgin o.o.—a travelling gourmet kit
—flavoring versus seasoning—the difference between herbs
and spices—an assemble-it-yourself aquavit!—don't knock
aunt bertha's american french dressing before you try it—
vinegar is a must*

7   desserts and more   116

*pastry is easy if you don't try too hard—a long overlooked
nanny-food worth looking up—virginia fried apples will
change your life—enjoy micro-fried granny-smiths—cornmeal
pancakes you'll really flip over—yankees can enjoy
spoonbread too—be the first on your block to sample a sines
pão-de-ló!*

8   in remembrance of meals past   129

*memorable meals on two continents from saddle of hare in a
paris bus station to a tantalizing tamale on the outskirts of
veracruz—a roast of larks in roquefort—the ultimate picnic,
un déjeuner sur l'herbe at the end of the world*

9   recipes that work   141

*55 dynamite recipes from acras to zucchini that work for me
and will work for you—in the unlikely event that you need
help with them, deeper discussions for most are made easy to
find by referring to their accompanying page numbers*

10   the index   173

all of the above, and then some—need i say more?

This book is dedicated

uncle Jack —

George Jacobs
10/25-/86

real cooking, by george!

1 | a beginning

Start here!

Most readers skip introductions but if you don't begin at this beginning, you might just have to eat your heart out instead of all the neat things I have in store for you.

Seems as though everyone who's not writing about sex these days is writing about food. Some of us derive great pleasure from the descriptions of exotic dishes we may never even get a chance to sample, let alone prepare. And people write about exotic dishes because there are only so many things one can say about ham and eggs. Unfortunately, exotic often translates into relative inaccessibility. The ingredients may be scarce, the expertise and/or patience required to prepare them might be in short supply, and the wonder-meals may turn out to be just too expensive.

Here's where *Real Cooking, by George* comes in. I've got some ways to deal with everyday food that will add zest to your eating. You don't have to live in a metropolis to take advantage of these ideas. Everything I talk about is available here and now. Granted, some elements like fresh vegetables are seasonal. And you may have to send off for a few delicacies like Virginia Ham, but the U.S. Mail is on hand to extend your culinary horizons to near infinity. I promise not to give you batches of off-the-wall preparations which have to start off with something that's been simmering on the back of the stove for the past three days.

If you are not into cooking, you can still enjoy reading about it. Gargantua said in 1554, "L'appétit vient en mangeant," appetite comes in eating. George says in 1986, "Appetite comes in reading about food, too."

power eating

Just about the time when would-be machos were no longer ashamed to admit that they not only knew what an avocado pear was but even ate them occasionally, along came the *Real Men Don't Eat Quiche* threat to masculinity. Now, it's *Power Lunching . . .* , another anti-hedonist killjoy.

It's no longer enough to wear the right clothes and drive the right car to and from the right address. The upwardly mobile person who wants to make it has to order the right things to eat in order to impress the right people.

Chewing this over, you might begin to think that I am on the power team. Not so. I am simply telling you all the things that I like to eat and suggesting that you try them too. My aim is to share, not intimidate. If some of the dishes I discuss strike your fancy, dig in. If something gives you indigestion just reading about it, skip to the next subject.

It helps to be aware of this insidious intimidation. Lord knows I've been menaced by it myself. I once had a hotel job which paid by the hour and included what was laughingly called lunch. It happened to be convenient for me, at the time, to go to work on a moped. Two wheels are not your real image builder, in the eyes of hotel staffers, unless they are holding up a heavy Harley. To compound my off-beat conduct, I carried my lunch in a waterproof Buck Rogers lunch box. I could deal with the pitying, sympathetic stares but not the house lunches.

The very first day I brought my own lunch to the staff cafeteria, I wound up with empty seats on either side of me. I mean, nobody wants to get too close to a weirdo. Right? But the ice broke when I opened the box. Its contents revealed a rib of roast pork (redolent of rosemary and garlic), an artichoke and a chunk of homemade Scotch shortbread. When I got to dipping one artichoke leaf at a time into oil and vinegar and obviously enjoying every morsel, the ambient condescension turned to curiosity. The crowd closed in, filled the adjacent seats and began to cadge samples. Come to think of it, I had come up with my own power lunch. From then on, I barely got in the door in the morning before I was asked what was on "our" menu for the day.

how to use this book

I want to share with you some of the fun I have had during my adventures in eating. You will soon know where I'm coming from but you'll also know how I got there. In my travels, whenever I found something I really liked, I found out as much as I could about it on the spot. What follows are some of the dishes that panned out when I tried them back home.

Not wishing to befuddle your bedside reading with a teaspoon of this and a cup of that, I'm giving, up front, outlines of what goes in and how to handle it as I go on about good things to eat. Then, if you start salivating and have to make a dash for the kitchen for relief, check the nuts & bolts section to the rear. There, you'll find bare bones recipes the way I like to find them when I'm chomping at the bit on the threshold of a new mouth-watering experience.

The first couple of times you try a recipe new to you, you might want to turn back to the text for tips on how to make it turn out right. Once you get the hang of a preparation, however, you won't want to have to wade through a story every time you want to find out what ingredients to include.

I've made all of the dishes for which I give recipes — they work for me. I hope you'll enjoy them as much as I do. And now, I have two important words for you: "LET'S PARTY!"

a garden party

Let me tell you about a party I threw to celebrate a messy roof remodeling. It took place in Portugal in 1964. I had bought a fisherman's cottage on the edge of an Algarvian cliff in Albufeira. To enjoy the spectacular view out over the Atlantic, I decided to add a second story. While constructing the forms and putting up the wire mesh for a cement floor, the workmen had converted the house interior to temporary shambles, decorated with shards of adobe and whitewash dust. This might not seem an appropriate time for quests but a happy occasion was in order to help me celebrate my victory over the red tape one encounters in getting building permits anywhere in the world.

It was in the middle of summer. The elements were kind and dining al fresco in my oceanfront garden was definitely the way to party. The main

problem besides the unesthetic interior rubble was removing cement flakes and splinters from the vicinity of eating materials. It wasn't the most convenient time to entertain but there were many interesting people in town who could be counted on to enjoy a different kind of "evening out." Among those on the invited list were our local Count, *O Conde de Marim y Alte* and his wife, mystery-men Len Deighton and Donald MacKenzie and their spouses, a charming Baroness from Germany, the mayor of Albufeira and other dear friends. I suggested that, due to the circumstances, they might prefer to leave their best bib and tucker at home and come prepared to rough it. What I had in mind was a cook-out where guests did the cooking.

Drinks were no problem. Back in the '60s, gin was a buck a bottle and local 16% wine was going for 75 cents a gallon. The salad course was easy to prepare and for dessert there was fruit, and there is no better fruit than that of Southern Portugal. The main course was, therefore, the only one which took any imagination. Charcoal cooking in Portugal was then the rule rather than the exception and every little mom and pop store sold charcoal stoves made of clay, shaped like hourglasses. These *fogareiros* cost less than a dollar apiece. Expecting ten couples, I bought four stoves and scrounged the rest from neighbors.

The morning of the party, I arranged to cut up what seemed like a whole lamb into one-inch cubes and put them to marinate in a large bowl. In went sliced onions, whole cloves of garlic, rosemary & thyme, bay leaves, pepper, a good ration of olive oil and some *colorau*. (*Colorau* is a spicy red powder along the lines of paprika. If you've ever tried to identify the special flavor of *linguiça*, Portuguese sausage, chances are it was *colorau*.) The heap was topped up with good strong local wine and covered over to rest (with occasional stirring) until evening.

The idea was that each couple would have a private stove and a plate of lamb chunks to roast on spits. The spits were new bicycle spokes, cheaper and much more available than anything else to use for shish kebabs. Once the inhibitions went down, closet chefs came out in strength. Everyone began skewering away with glee. I had laid on a mound of *Papsecos*, Portuguese rolls which look like bulkies but are 36,000 times better. Once a spit of meat was grilled to suit its chef, it was inserted between two halves of a *papseco* and the spoke was withdrawn for another round.

If you want to experiment and don't care for lamb, try this with beef. Lamb in Europe seems to be milder and more delicious to some of us. I don't use it often here. As for the *fogareiros*, you can use small hibachis from the discount stores where they can be purchased for not much more than their Portuguese cousins. Keep plenty of paper napkins on hand and let the red wine flow.

I've had my share of interesting parties here and abroad. Sometimes it's been only a party of one, but good things to eat make up for a lot of dull company. So, whether you're alone or in company, enjoy food. If the larder is bare, read about it. Don't deprive your visitors, either. Leave a second copy of this book on the night-stand in the guest room.

off to an early start

My interest in things good to eat dates back to the days when I grew tall enough to open the ice-box door and pilfer butter balls, which I liked better than candy. In those days of the Depression, our family grew to appreciate the finer edibles because my mother had to launch a home-catering business to make ends meet. The food which was most in demand was *gourmet* because those who could afford to entertain bought only the best and that's what Mom turned out. We enjoyed regional cooking, from the region of Virginia mainly. The slogan of Mother's establishment: *Virginia Recipes— Foods for the Sophisticate.*

My paternal ancestors were no slouches when it came to matters of the table. Dad was from the fringes of Pennsylvania-Dutch country. For those who haven't had the pleasure, put this area on your gastronomic map. It is one of the few areas left where the tradition of good eating has maintained standards of excellence. The local produce is superb. Generous measures of t.l.c. accompany cooking in all aspects. Food is hearty, ample and delicious. Not a few recipes from my father's Yankee mother crept into the file of

"Virginia Recipes." I remember my grandmother at the helm of her huge coal stove, which burned from dawn to dusk. When she wasn't roasting local livestock and simmering vegetables, she was turning out cookies and pies. The thought of them still makes me hungry.

In those days, one ate what was in season. Seasonal food always seems better *if it's local*, and when it is, the tendency is still for one to o.d. on treats like asparagus and strawberries. This heavy sampling makes it easier to wait for next year's repeat performance.

For me, even butter had its season, as I recall. When spring came along, country butter often reeked of the wild onions Bossie was prone to nibble. As a kid, I couldn't handle the butter when it tasted like sour towels. Boy, what I wouldn't give for some good country butter now—maybe even with the onions.

Before our rapid transportation worked up to its current frenzy, there wasn't the huge variety of victuals now available almost anywhere. Even so, living in farm country didn't necessarily mean that folks took advantage of everything available. For example, in Dad's hometown loads of farmers raised and/or hunted ducks, but they never made it to the menu in his family. This I discovered at about age ten during a household trauma. My mother had roasted a duck for my father as a surprise when he came home from the office. His reaction was twofold. "Get that deformed chicken out of my sight!" he shouted and then marched upstairs, not to be seen until much later. Talk about male chauvinism . . .

On the other hand, my mother came from a staunch Methodist clan. Abstemious would best describe its attitude toward fermented beverages. The family legend has it that my father produced a bottle of wine at the beginning of my parents' honeymoon and that my mother poured it down the sink. Incidents like this and the pall of Prohibition guided me through a rather sheltered childhood. I do remember times when the bathtub was commandeered for some mysterious alchemy not related to soap, but it suited me just fine to forgo a session in the suds.

By the time I was nearly old enough to drink, I was in a Quaker college (Haverford) where moderation prevailed. Moderation there, in matters alcoholic, would have mollified the Methodists I'm sure. In fact I had no more than a passing acquaintance with the pleasures of drink until I went abroad in my mid-twenties. Once subjected to the ubiquity of wine and other nice nectars, I began to make up for lost time and haven't quit since.

the french connection

My tastebuds went international when I moved to France in 1951. That country was still recuperating from the war but the French were already eating high on the hog in spite of economic chaos and generally rundown amenities. The English, at that time, were lucky to have an egg a week and those who could afford to, would take the cross channel *French* ferries just to gorge on meat and butter on board. It was after my first channel crossing that I found out about the Michelin Guide and became fascinated with the fascination of the French for food.

Living on the French economy, it took me a while, but I eventually scraped together enough francs to buy a motor-scooter. My new wheels enabled me to make a tour of France, Austria and Germany with a tent and Bonny, my faithful Skye Terrier. We shared many meals over a camp stove but whenever we came near a three-star restaurant in France, I tethered the dog to the scooter and went inside to splurge. The greatest treat of them all was near Lyons, in Vienne, at the *Restaurant de la Pyramide*.

To many *La Pyramide* is still the most famous of all French restaurants. At that time, it was still benefiting from the presence and benign touches of its owner, Fernand Point, whose name is nearly always preceded by "The legendary." I still remember it all . . .

The restaurant was set well back from the highway in a grove of stately trees and carefully manicured shrubbery. There were splashes of gold and crimson flowers and a few lawn chairs for those who chose to linger for an apéritif. Seeing was only part of the thrill. Through the open dining-room

windows, I heard the gentle clink of crystal and inhaled the rich perfume of butter and cream and fine wine. My mouth turned to water and I was still outdoors.

I was received in my rough traveling get-up just as warmly as any three-pieced client with big francs to spend. There was hardly an empty seat but I was given a window table where I could keep an eye on Bonny. I was astounded at how so many happy diners could make so little noise. They were too busy eating and purring to break into loud conversation. There wasn't a cigarette in sight. I had strolled into an impressionist painting come to life.

Following the Michelin Guide's suggestions, I ordered fish and chicken and "house" wine. The fish was *Truites Farçies Braisées au Porto*. When trout becomes *truite*, it's no longer pieces of fish dipped in cornmeal and done over a campfire. I was presented with an entire *truite*, boned, stuffed and braised in Port wine. It was nestling in parsley on a long silver platter for my approval. Just one whiff was enough to launch my memorable meal. I could only guess at the contents of the stuffing and sauce. Some things are better left a tasty mystery.

The "house" wine, incidentally, was a *Meursault* and the only way it resembled the usual house wine was that it came in an unlabelled bottle. The same may be said for the red which was *Moulin-à-Vent*, long since a favorite Beaujolais of mine. Such splendid vintages appearing in nondescript containers is rather like having our President appear before Congress in overalls.

The chicken was *La Volaille de Bresse à la Crème. Volaille* is a two-dollar word for fowl carefully raised for eating and *Bresse* is an eastern region of France where they wrote the book on how it's done. My serving was an entire small chicken, boned and reassembled, slathered with unctuous creamy nectar, lightly perfumed with herbs and wine. The only caution to be observed in eating either of these courses was to avoid wolfing them down.

A light green salad followed by a tray of cheeses completed my menu. It was all I could do to struggle back to the scooter. Needless to say, I took a few moments repose in the patio to reflect on my adventure and gather equilibrium to face the next stage of my journey. It was obvious to me that I wouldn't have to eat again for days, at least not feast.

Note to fellow dog-lovers: I mentioned to one of my waiters that there was a three-star dog waiting for me in the garden and that if a filet of something had fallen to the floor, perhaps I could take it out to her between courses. "Pas de problème, Monsieur, votre tou-tou va être bien traité." From my window-side table I could see one of the staff carrying out a covered dish treat, making Bonny as happy as her master. It was a bit of boeuf bourguignon I was told. Quite a far cry from a doggie-bag, I'd say.

Though I have rarely enjoyed such complete perfection since, I have not

given up sampling and learning. After several years in France, where I lived with French families or alone, I gradually migrated south to spend time in Spain and eventually settled in Portugal. While not on a par with French cuisine, Iberian reserves some memorable moments for those daring enough to go outside standard *International Hotel* food. The Portuguese are a little more interested in fine food than the Spanish, but at all levels of society they both offer lavish food and superior service that is difficult to locate, at any price, in our land of fast food.

In the sixties, Bonny and I ate our way across the United States and finally down into Mexico. By then we were traveling by camper, a Commer Caravan from England. It was a lot more comfortable than the scooter and much easier to cook in than the tent. One or the other of us sampled spiced round in Mississippi (delicious), catfish in Louisiana (forgettable), Tex-Mex in Texas, and *real* Mex in Mexico where that kind of food should be eaten and enjoyed.

Much of the excitement of such a trip is furnished by the quality of local specialties which change with the scenery. Eating in ordinary restaurants was not interesting until I experienced Mexico. One dazzling exception was of course New Orleans fare. There, however, my means did not permit the extravagant sampling of gastronomic finery that I had been able to afford in Europe.

In these days of high restaurant prices and unpredictable quality, your best eating can be done at home. I am offering you food based on what I have cooked and enjoyed in my own kitchen. There are dishes I learned to appreciate while growing up, as well as those I came to learn about and love through travel. I am drawing on the food of France, Spain, and Portugal. For those who enjoy something really different, I'm passing along palate pleasers experienced in the French Caribbean, where some of the best of both sides of the Atlantic has melded into an art form.

2 | first courses and such

Life in the fast lane has changed eating habits in many ways, most of them objectionable to me. Fast food operations lay a whole meal on us in one swoop. For some, TV dinners almost spelled finis to multi-course meals. Although not a new habit, taking strong drink before eating has made subtle tastes difficult to cultivate. Obviously, not everyone has the time or the resources to sit down to a complicated spread every time the dinner bell rings. However, splitting an average evening meal into courses can make life a lot more interesting and, dare I say it, even more healthful in some ways. Convenience is one aspect of life—pleasure is another. I condone convenience but I prefer pleasure in matters gastronomic.

Salad is a favorite course of mine, as long as it's not the first one. It's become the custom in restaurants for a small overloaded bowl of bunny-food to be plonked down on the table way before the main dish.

There are lots of good reasons for this, seen from the point of view of anyone but the diner. Salad is not expensive and toying with it gives the eater something to do while waiting for an order to penetrate to the kitchen and give the chef time to get his shift together. All the waiter or waitress has to do is slosh the requested dressing on some tired greens and away you go. Many restaurants have eliminated even this duty by setting up elaborate salad bars at which you help yourself. This saves manpower and gives us a wider choice. I like my greens at the end of the meal but this is a losing battle. Given that we have become accustomed to this procedure, therefore, I have a few suggestions for something a little different to launch a lunch or dinner. Maybe you'll care to try them.

crudités, **a refined appetizer**

Crudités is French for raw things—usually vegetables and occasionally fruit —served as an appetizer. An American version of this kind of appetizer is reflected in the salad bars which are springing up all over the country.

Crudités taste much better than the word sounds. Thin strings of carrots, for example, with either oil and vinegar or mayonnaise will perk up anyone's appetite. Many inexpensive French restaurants offer dishes like this as a first course. Fancy French restaurants do too but they use a fancier name and charge more. *Crudités* may include such things as cucumbers, cabbage, radishes, celery root and the like, sliced, grated or whole and enhanced with some kind of dressing. The raw ingredients are relatively inexpensive and almost always in season. They are a handy preparation to be familiar with, especially when unexpected guests show up.

If you haven't sprung for a food processor yet, you can always use the old faithful trapezoidal steel contraption. A happy compromise is the French *MOULI-JULIENNE* (short for *moulin,* French for mill, and julienne which means, roughly, diced). That's the gadget on the right. It comes with five disks and will make light work of many dishes like shoestring potatoes and potato-chips. I'll have other suggestions for a *mouli* as we go along. They run by hand and cost anywhere from five to fifteen dollars, depending on how chic a shop you buy them from.

Either peel or scrub the outside of the carrots, cut into manageable pieces and grate or put through the mill using one of the fine, but not the finest, disks. Put the shreds into a bowl and add oil and vinegar plus salt and

mouli-julienne

pepper if you wish. There is probably no easier-to-prepare first course short of opening a can of something prepared in a faraway fast-food factory.

If you prefer, instead of oil and vinegar, use mayonnaise, which is as good or better, provided it's not the usual commercial glop. The recipe in this book will make you give up the bottled brands for keeps.

The cucumbers can be sliced or grated. The French go through a long rigamarole of grating, salting, and putting a weighted cloth on top to get the water to drain off. I prefer them thinly sliced, accompanied by small slivers of onions, oil and vinegar and a hint of sugar, especially if the onions are strong. Letting the combination sit around a bit with a few ice cubes on top will crisp up the ensemble.

Grated cabbage, treated in the same way as the carrots, is less delicate but delicious in small doses. You might want to drip in some Worcestershire or soy sauce for added zip. Cabbage is not all that exciting unless it comes straight from your garden. It can be made more colorful if you use both red and green, and if you are desperate for taste enhancement, grate in a touch of turnip with a radish or two.

Some Chinese restaurants offer Szechuan cabbage. I tried duplicating the dish at home by shredding cabbage and flavoring it with rice wine and slivers of ginger. It was close enough and very appetizing.

If you are fortunate enough to be in an area where they sell celery root (celeriac), then you can whip up the most refined *crudité* north of the Caribbean and west of Brittany. To give the celery root the ultimate flavor fillip, mix in a bit of hot mustard like Colemans dry, or a wet brand you are fond of. Mustard is important in this dish. Not only does it improve the flavor but it tenderizes the celery strands, making them less difficult to eat. The French call this *celeri remoulade* though the term *remoulade* can vary considerably and cover a multitude of dishes. The word is from an old Picardy term, *ramolas*, meaning horseradish, not a bad optional addition to the *crudité* department.

Some of the exotic roots they wing your way in the Caribbean are delightful the first few times you sample them. If you eat in simple Caribbean or French restaurants, you'll get all too familiar with the same *crudités*, but from time to time they are more than just acceptable. *Christophines* come to mind as examples of a very tasty vegetable-member of the cucumber family found all over the Caribbean. World travelers may have run into them as *chouchoutes* in Polynesia or Madagascar. In Mexico, they are known as *chayotes*. Down south in our own country they are called *mirlitons*. No matter what they're called, *Christophines* are good eating, raw or cooked.

As a rule of thumb, if the main dish is expensive for a restaurant to produce, you will often be served a huge heap of *crudités* in the hopes that you will overindulge and not leave too much room for the more expensive *pièce de résistance*. Don't worry—the French will not let you leave the table hungry and there will always be enough of something else to please you if this form of appetizer leaves you cold. You can rest assured that *crudités* will continue to grow in popularity in the U.S. now that everybody is into raw and roughage.

anchovies & endive

The ease of preparation of anchovies and endive as a first course is exceeded only by the surprised delight of its lucky eaters. It helps if anchovies are not on the list of things you can't stand, but I've had raves from dyed-in-the-linen anti-anchovites, *before* they realized what they were eating. As for the endive itself, I am referring to *Belgian* endive as opposed to a variety of escarole. The former is shaped like a ship and the latter like a chartreuse afro. If it helps, pronounce the Belgian kind "on deeve" where the "on" is like the "on" in "honk" and escarole variety as "en dive." In supermarkets like the ones on Cape Cod, where not all the sales personnel are familiar with it, it sometimes helps to remind them to look under the "B's" for Belgian endive so that the check-out computer can take over from there.

Allow a small endive per person and a tin of anchovies for three or four people. Rinse off the endive but leave each one whole. Put the anchovies in a small saucepan and place over a medium heat. In a matter of minutes, the little fish will no longer be recognizable. They will have changed from long skinny little skeletons to a puddle of succulent sauce. (If you use the ones with capers, the little seeds will still be whole and for this reason, many prefer the flat fish without the garnish.) Ration out the sauce into little cups and put one on each plate with the endive next to it. If you are into artichokes, you won't have any problem figuring out how to consume this delicacy. Peel off the endive leaves one at a time and dip the ends into the juice. Allow the surplus to drip off and chomp. Second and third dips per leaf are recommended as they grow shorter.

If you are a real anchovy freak, and there are some of us who are, you might find that one tin won't stretch to more than two people. Don't be greedy though. Remember that thirst is brought to a head by eating salt and anchovies are loaded with it. Too many can spoil the rest of a meal by causing you to fill up on liquid refreshment.

This is finger-food so no silverware is necessary. Napkins are, however. Served with fine crystal under candlelight, this appetizer will transport you to Lucullan heights.

the avocado

One of the most satisfying quick meals for me is an avocado. It requires a minimum of preparation, tastes good, is very nourishing and it's cheap. What used to be a somewhat effete luxury item is now available much of the year at a price within anyone's budget. While avocados are not to everyone's taste, I think they would be enjoyed by more people if they knew what to do with them. All too often, they are gussied up with some exotic stuffing like crab salad which overpowers their natural suave taste. I learned how good they are plain on the island of Madeira, where street vendors sell them as snacks. They found in me a willing customer. I would shell out an escudo or two for a ripe avocado, slice it in two, peel the halves and let the pieces melt in my mouth. One was enough to get me through half a day. Before I reveal more sophisticated treatments of this marvelous fruit, a bit of avocado lore is in order.

Considered a fruit by some and a vegetable by others, avocados are native to the tropical Americas, where they have been a staple for over 6,000 years. (They arrived in Florida from Mexico in 1833.) Because of their (sometimes) rough skin and pendant shape, they are also called "alligator pears." The word avocado comes via the Spanish from the Aztec language of Nahuatl. The Indian word *ahuacatl* was hung on the fruit for the same reason that the Greeks used *orkhis* for the orchid—both words mean testicle in their respective languages and in those days, people called things the way they saw them.

Where avocados grow in profusion, they have become very much a part of the daily diet, often as not some version of guacamole. This is another word from Nahuatl, *gahuacamolli*, meaning avocado sauce. (That's where that word *mole* you see on Mexican restaurant menus originated—it just means sauce.) With or without added seasonings, mashed avocado is often spread on tortillas or bread the way we would do with butter. There are so many recipes for guacamole floating around that I won't bother to add to the confusion, except for this tip: If you make it up a bit ahead of time, you can help the guacamole keep its color by leaving the pits in the bowl with it. You can even serve it that way.

Compared to other vegetable-fruits, the avocado is long on B vitamins and oil (we're talking 20% FAT!), and short on sugar and vitamins A and C. The latter characteristic incites the sweet-toothed Brazilians to add sugar to theirs and call it fruit. In any form, avocados are filling and go a long way towards warding off starvation. It's advisable to avoid counting calories when indulging. Avocadoes will blow away your calculator.

In my oft-thwarted searches to purchase an already ripe avocado in the North, I have long been laboring under a false impression. I concluded that the rock-hard pears available at the market were just other victims of the food industry, which causes growers to pick unripe foods for shipping ease— never mind the tasteless results for the consumer.

Much to my surprise, I finally learned that, unlike most fruits, avocadoes will *not* ripen on the tree unless their skins are split. Apparently they "mature" on the tree but they don't ripen on the branch. Once picked, however, they begin to turn edible and will go on ripening unless deprived of air. Therefore, if you stumble upon an avocado ready to eat when you're not, cut off its air supply by wrapping it up tightly in a plastic bag. When you and the pear are ready, unwrap and eat, for it will soon spoil once the oxygen gets back to it.

Do not—repeat, DO NOT—put it in the refrigerator, a mistake I used to make before I saw the light. When subjected to cold, the avocado will not only turn brown and stringy inside but begin to taste funny too. As a visual clue, the skin on the alligator-patterned ones turns dark purple, almost black, when the insides are ready—the shiny green ones stay green even after they begin to spoil. When you are shopping for them, you can tell by the feel if they are too ripe. The feel can be deceiving, however. Some hard ones are o.k.; some barely soft are rotten. By shaking one, you can occasionally judge its condition by whether or not the pit rattles around. If it does and the pear isn't soft, chances are that it's ready. If in doubt, get several, especially when they're only 3 for 89 cents, a frequently seen price in season, which goes from the first of the year to around April if you live far from the avocado orchards.

As I recall, during my youth I got the distinct impression that rigid-wristed men just didn't eat avocados except possibly to humor their wives behind closed doors. I wonder if it would have taken so long for them to become "acceptable" had we gringos been instructed in the finer points of the Peruvian avocado festival which may be still going on for all I know. In the good old days, at least, when the pears were about ready to pick, all men and boys went on short rations for five days. After five days of abstemious behavior, during which they refrained from salt, pepper and carnal bliss, they gathered, starkers, amidst the avocado trees to perform their version of "The bare went over the mountain." Their ritual granted open season on any distaff who wandered across their path. Females who did so were promptly violated on the spot. This performance was supposed to mellow the pears! For quite some time, the avocado has been considered an aphrodisiac and perhaps this is the reason for the mellowing ritual. (For further details, see Sir James G. Frazer, *The Golden Bough*, Macmillan and Co.)

As good as those Madeira pears were on the sidewalk, they could be improved upon. If I resisted temptation long enough to get them back near the kitchen, I used to eat them with olive oil, vinegar and a few shavings of garlic. When sliced in halves and pitted, they formed natural receptacles for this simple vinaigrette, mixed in the shell, as it were. I would slightly score the flesh to let the sauce penetrate and then ladle out spoonfuls directly to my mouth. However, not everyone around the house will settle for this simplified treatment. When I arrive home from market with avocados, the first question I'm asked is: "Did you buy grapefruit too?" For us, grapefruit and avocados are as closely intertwined on the family food chain as black-eyed peas and stewed tomatoes or fried apples and bacon. I must confess that the combination is one on which our often divergent points of view definitely converge. The two form the basis of a superb salad which I mention along with Aunt Bertha's French dressing. See page 110.

eggs

There are lots of good first courses which are based on eggs. Eggs Benedict, curried eggs, omelets, shirred, etc. The French often offer *oeufs à la mayonnaise*—hard-boiled with mayo. Some of these depend on knowing how to boil an egg and, strange to say, not everyone is clued in on the fine points of egg boiling.

Back in the days of our family food business near Philadelphia, there were still a few stuffy Main Line matrons sufficiently untouched by the Depression to vaunt the fact that they didn't even know how to boil an egg. Well, most of their domestics have gone the way of the dinosaur and such professed ignorance of matters culinary has virtually vanished too. Few people now admit to not knowing their way around the kitchen but there are still many people who actually don't know how to boil an egg the RIGHT way!

Actually, the absolutely right way is still a matter of dispute and the consensus is that there is no consensus. Assuming that you start out with a good egg—i.e., fresh and uncracked—there are at least three things that can go wrong in hard-boiling: (1) the egg can crack and get messy looking while losing some of its white; (2) you can wind up with that unattractive gray-green layer around the yolk, leading consumers to conclude that the egg wasn't fresh, which is not necessarily true; or (3) the result can turn out too soft or too tough.

Here are some of the solutions I've uncovered after heavy research and a fair amount of experience:

To avoid the cracking, try to start with eggs at room temperature as opposed to putting them directly into a hot pot from the cold refrigerator. This is necessary only when you have an egg with a hairline fracture or worse. Actually, an unblemished egg can go from a bowl of ice and water and be plunged directly into boiling water without a scar! The catch is that the egg has to be perfect—and few things are these days.

Laying aside the cracking question, there is a sharp division of theory as to the best way to boil. Some suggest placing the eggs into already boiling water; others recommend putting the eggs in tap-temperature water and bringing the ensemble to a boil. If you are a pre-boiling person, you may have already had the tell-tale white sneak out of the shell. You can reduce the chances of this happening in several ways, they say. The French solution is the simplest—put plenty of salt in the water. A more finicky method is to punch small holes in the ends of the eggs, and gadgets actually exist for this purpose. People pay money for these things which do no better job than an ordinary pin, should you wish to experiment. These holes are to let the air (instead of the white) escape from inside the egg when heat hits the interior.

I expect to survive without an egg-holer, but one of them could be a conversation starter to give to the cook who has everything—well, nearly everything.

You can also add vinegar to the water. This may not always stop the cracking but it will keep the escaped white from going all over the pot.

Conclusion: the easiest way is to start with eggs *and* water at room-temperature.

Next comes the problem of the funky yolk. To maintain a pristine yellow throughout—i.e., without that green-gray exterior—put the eggs in cold water *immediately* when you have decided that they have cooked long enough. If the shells haven't cracked already, give them a rap. Let the cold water seep in to cool them faster and make them easier to shuck.

The proper length of time to hard-boil an egg is a highly subjective matter. It depends on the size of the egg, the cold or boiling water approach, and the taste of the egg-eater. Try using cold water, bring it and the eggs to a boil, and remove from heat, leaving a cover on the pan during the whole operation. Wait about 10 minutes more and transfer the eggs to cold water. Timing is least critical by this method, which makes it a good one to use when you are doing several other things at the same time. This way will also prevent tough whites as well as cut down on the chances of that green skin on the yolk, both of which can result from prolonged boiling.

If you want to use the already-boiling method, slide the eggs into the bath and leave them there from 12 to 20 minutes according to size. Then, put them into the cold water and they are ready when you want them.

Hard-boiled eggs are at their best, for me, when deviled or as some would say "stuffed." After cooling, they are cut in half lengthwise. The yolk is mixed with mayonnaise and mustard with a shot of Worcestershire sauce and put back into the hardened egg white halves. If you are preparing a big batch for a party, rotate the eggs occasionally while they are cooking so that the yolk will wind up in the middle of the egg and look roundly happy on the canapé tray. There are plenty of other ways to make use of hard-boiled eggs and you probably have your favorites. When driving more than 25 miles, Colleen, my nephew's mother-in-law, would rather leave home without her American Express card than a supply of hard-boiled eggs. I agree with her to the extent that they sure beat turnpike pitstops to stave off starvation.

gazpacho

There are some forty million people in Spain and twenty-five million ways to make gazpacho. (Children under 6 don't do much in the kitchen except eat.) The first time I tasted this delicious cold soup was in the Barcelona Ritz in

1951. The luxurious surroundings would never have led me to believe that this is what a lot of people in Spain ate when they couldn't afford much of anything else—a condition which, I am happy to say, has changed considerably for the better since those post-war days.

Magazines have accustomed us to seeing gazpacho presented in a bowl with croutons and chopped vegetables floating around. That's the way it was in the Ritz, so you can imagine my surprise when I ordered it in Córdoba and was served a beer glass full of white liquid. Since tomatoes are a principal ingredient of gazpacho as we know it, I asked the waiter if he had really served me gazpacho. Yes, indeed he had, he explained—I was drinking "Gazpacho del Rio." Further investigation revealed that the "river gazpacho" was something like "Chateau de la Pompe," which the French use to mean water or very-watered wine. The rio, or river, indicated that the gazpacho was mostly water and the white, thick look came from dry Spanish white bread, whiter than which there is nothing short of chalk. The concoction relied almost exclusively for taste upon garlic. I loved it and had two more glasses on the spot.

When the garden finally makes up its mind to ripen tomatoes, I turn to gazpacho for a nice summer starter. I reduce cucumbers, bell peppers, onions, garlic and tomatoes to pieces small enough to fit easily into the blender. Next, I throw in lashings of olive oil to get the morsels afloat, blend away, adding salt and pepper and maybe a little more water if I'm using strong oil and don't want its flavor to overpower the soup. Pieces of stale bread add consistency and stretch the quantity. Actually, this is pretty close to one of Phyllis Diller's meatless garbage soups except that I think she heats hers. The whole idea of gazpacho is to have it cold and, when time allows, the above would go into the refrigerator to get icy cold. When I require instant gazpacho gratification, I add no water; instead, I whirl in ice cubes just long enough for them to dissolve but not lose their cool. This is great as is, but if you want to pull out all the stops, sliced, diced rations of the ingredients plus croutons will convert a bowl of this into a dish worthy of the Barcelona or any other Ritz.

pâté anyone?

Before I slip too far into the soups, I want to mention pâtés. The literal meaning of pâté is "paste" but it has become a catch-all term for anything from yesterday's meat loaf to a velvety melding of *foie gras* (which is French for fat liver, a definition which doesn't sound nearly as appetizing in English). Yes, we've been eating pâté for generations without realizing it because meat loaf could be considered *pâté de campagne* (country pâté). This is a coarse French concoction of meat and spices, served cold with *cornichons*, sour little French pickles that take some getting used to. The main difference

I'd like to skip lunch today — my liver is acting up.

between meat loaf and pâté, besides ingredients, is one's state of mind. Meat loaf makes one think of beer, pâté evokes Champagne. I don't care for meat loaf until its second day, and then I usually find it very good — cold — with spicy sauce instead of gravy. That's the way pâté is always eaten — cold.

Regardless of any other ingredients involved, pâté *does* have more fat in its make-up than meat loaf — up to one-third of the total ingredients! That's what the breadcrumbs are doing in it, absorbing the fat and keeping the whole pâté from drying out. Many meat loaf recipes also call for breadcrumbs. Hamburger which is not ultra-lean demands their use for similar reasons. Too much beef fat is bad news in either. It hardens into little beads. Pork fat is not only suaver but it tastes better too.

Often on French menus, you'll see *Pâté de Foie Gras*. This is liver paste. It can be delicious or it can be ho-hum. It should not be confused with *Foie Gras d'Oie*, which specifies that the liver come from a force-fed goose and costs like smoke. It is available in the U.S. tinned — unless you live in the kind of area where it might be flown in from France for special occasions.

This deluxe liver is rich and stultifying to taste buds. By that I mean that it is most enjoyable to consume but what you eat next will seem bland by comparison. A worldly host will serve the real thing only at the end of a meal in order not to interfere with more subtle dishes. Regular pâtés are usually less overpowering as starters. When I am fortunate enough to come by genuine *Foie Gras*, I make a whole meal out of it — with bread and wine. Never mind any further trimmings.

In fancy restaurants, the term *terrine* pops up in reference to pâtés. A *terrine* is the glazed clay vessel in which some pâtés are made and served. Take away the *terrine* and you've got pâté.

I used to make pâtés frequently. Butchers were more obliging and it was easier then than now to get the meats one wanted ground to order. Well, I'm back in the pâté groove now, thanks to a food processor. I put off buying one for a long time. I have nothing against hi-tech. It's just that there is already so much hardware in our kitchen that it looks like a branch of the flea market. It would have been less than fair, I rationalized, to put this book together without sharing the advantages of such a marvel. So, I bit the bullet and bought one. The very first thing I made with it was — you guessed it — a pâté.

The essential ingredients of a simple "country" pâté are meat(s), spices, a spot of brandy or wine, and an egg or two to hold things together. American-French cookbooks don't make much mention of breadcrumbs but French-French cookbooks do. I figure if using breadcrumbs is good enough for the French, I can live with them too. Putting all these things together by hand is quite feasible but it's a whole lot easier with a processor.

Here's what I do: I cut up an onion, peel a few cloves of garlic, moisten some breadcrumbs with milk and process them briefly with an egg. I add ground pepper and a few whole peppercorns, rosemary, thyme and whatever else I have a hankering for at the time. If I have bought my meats already ground, I add them to the machine and blend the whole works until the only whole thing left is the peppercorns. If you have bought your meat in chunks, you might have an easier time emptying out the first ingredients so that you can have better control over grinding up pork, veal, beef, liver or what-have-you. Once the meat is homogeneous, back in go the spices and things for a brief final blending.

The longer you process the meat, the finer the texture will be. Some like crumbly pâtés on the order of meat loaf. I like it denser. Since this is going to be eaten cold, possibly even as a sandwich, the firmer pâté slices and handles better.

Line your terrine with thin slices of salt pork or some other fat of your choice. Pile in the mixture and stick a bay leaf on top, lightly embedded. Put the *terrine* in a pan of water and then into the oven at 350 degrees. I use a soufflé dish or a crock to hold the pâté and a roasting pan to hold the crock. One and a half to two hours will do a three pound pâté to perfection. Some cooks like to cover the pâté with foil but I prefer to leave the top exposed so I can smell and watch it better. It's done when the juice bubbling around it is no longer pink. Although it is not essential, a weight placed on top of the pâté while it is cooling will make it more uniform in texture and easier to slice. Start digging in on the second or third day.

Remember, this is an ultra-simple version. You can make it more complicated by sautéing the onions first, mincing the garlic, hiding pickles or truffles in the interior but it won't make that much better a pâté. Keep it down to the bare essentials. Just the satisfaction of having created your own

pâté will render its simplicity that much more satisfying. Later on, if you get bored, you can start pulling out fancier stops.

If you don't have a processor, don't fret. Buy the meats already ground and mix the daylights out of everything.

blackbean soup

My most favorite soup is black bean. To be made properly—i.e., the way I like it—Virginia ham squeezings are required. Virginia ham comes up a little later on but there's no harm in peeking ahead if you want to know what's in stock for you, as it were . . .

As often as not, good soups are by-products of some other kitchen delight. Gone, for the time being, are the days when the stock pot simmered at the back of the stove at home, and more's the pity, because many resort to store-bought soups which get worse every time they are "improved." Frugal and clever cooks make the most of leftover bones and roasting juices but if you've gone to the trouble of fixing up a real Virginia ham, you'll have enough ham stock left to make gallons of good, hearty soup. You'll see what this entails in the next section. If you don't choose to go whole hog and do your own ham, you can buy smoked ham shanks in the supermarket and use them. A short time in a pressure cooker (with water, of course) will ensure maximum flavor for the basic broth. If no shanks are to be found, you can use a piece of smoked pork butt.

Basic black is my first choice but with slight alterations, the following recipe for it can net you a full spectrum of other tasty bean creations. There's white bean, yellow and green split pea, lentil and kidney bean—they all work out well.

Black beans are somewhat scarce in New England but I have found them in health food and gourmet shops. For 6 to 8 quarts of soup, invest in about 3 pounds of black beans. Here's how to finagle two favorites on the fire at the same time:

When you put the ham to soak in cold water overnight, do the same with the 3 pounds of black beans (in a separate pot). This way you will be able to brew up at least one batch of soup right after you boil the ham the following day. The ham-boiling procedure is discussed in the meat section. You'll have to refer to it if you are making this soup the traditional way.

Siphon off about 2 quarts from the boiler—the ham broth, *not* the water the ham spent the night in. Freeze the rest for later use. Finely chop about a pound of onions with celery—use two parts onion to one part celery. Heat them until soft in either a little bit of fat (like salt pork or bacon grease) or just plain ham broth. Drain and rinse the beans. Put in 4 quarts of water and add vegetables along with the ham juice. Toss in a bay leaf or two, some salt and pepper and simmer away.

For maximum flavor, wrestle the ham hock loose and put that in too. If you don't take out the whole bone, saw off the protruding end. The second and third time around, you can use more of the bone from which you will have by then sliced away the ham. It won't be quite as powerful as the whole hock so you can add some of the less manageable pieces of meat and fat which accumulate as you work your way through the ham. I save them for just this purpose.

After two or three hours at low heat, the *simmering* soup will be done. Remove the bone(s) and try to fish out the bay leaf if it hasn't disintegrated. Put the whole business through the blender or food processor. Never fill these machines more than half full with this kind of mixture. This will avoid unpleasant side-effects such as redecorating your ceiling. When the blending is over, mix the whole lot together for uniform consistency and freeze what you can't eat the first time. Tradition says serve with slices of hard-boiled egg, lemon wedges and a dollop of sherry per bowl. I add to tradition by floating a spoonful of sour cream on my share. With a few pieces of buttered toast and a glass of red wine, a body can fill up with pleasure. It is easy to go overboard on black bean soup so don't eat quite all you want. One bowl will do it.

If you prefer to look at the beans while you are eating the soup, blend only a part of what you have cooked and use it to thicken the rest.

Note: If you use split peas instead of black beans, your soup can cook in about an hour, but many prefer to let it keep on simmering until it gets

mushy enough so that it doesn't have to be puréed. Split pea soup doesn't get along all that well with the garnishings recommended for black bean except for the sour cream. As a welcome addition, float a few crunchy croutons on top at the last minute.

start with spaghetti?

In the United States, we are accustomed to thinking of spaghetti as a meal in itself. In all but Italian neighborhoods, we have been serving it with a meat and tomato sauce, too. There's still hardly a school in the country that doesn't ring in "Spaghetti and meatballs" on its weekly menus.

There *are* other ways to fix it and, in moderate doses, it makes a good opening dish instead of the main course. Minced garlic in hot butter with a little rosemary is one of my favorites. Butter and shredded Swiss cheese marry happily with spaghetti. Shucks, it's good with just olive oil and some of the stronger Italian cheeses, grated on top. If unexpected guests drop in, you can stretch a previously planned small dinner into a big enough meal by starting off with a first course of spaghetti in one of these easy and quick ways. Keep a couple of cans of clam sauce on the shelf for just such occasions. There are good ones on the market which will taste better after you add some garlic and spices to them. This is much easier than starting a clam sauce from scratch.

hard at work cooking
dinner in Chanzeauy

Another combination I use relies on the Virginia ham I keep talking about. Little scraggly ends of it (with the fat left on) warmed in butter with a splash of sherry and some sprigs of rosemary can be brought together while the pasta is in the pot. Just before serving, put a liberal amount of sour cream in the ham and things and heat to bubbling—no hotter. That mixed with steaming spaghetti will make your reputation and ruin your friends' diets. Better reserve that one for a whole meal (with salad, natch).

Slightly more conventional is the regular presentation that we are all used to. Here's a little personal twist to it:

We are always happy when we can pry my niece away from bustling Boston for a week-end with us down on quiet Cape Cod. Not only do we enjoy her company but it also means we get a legitimate excuse to serve spaghetti. Solid but sylphlike, she can eat all of us under the table in short order, especially when the main dish is spaghetti. Her brother is no dieter in this department and when the two of them show up together, we resident trenchermen have to get out the biggest pot in the house to stave off starvation. About the only thing worse than a power failure of a Friday night visit (we have electric stoves, alas) is when we run out of the succulent sauce my mother puts up by the gallon when peppers and tomatoes are in season. These two guests are as finicky as they are voracious and a run-of-the-mill store-bought sauce would play havoc with our usually happy family harmony.

A shortage was bound to happen sooner or later and when it did one blustery evening last winter, I had to come to the rescue with a trick I discovered back when I was living alone on what might be called a restricted budget. I was shifting for myself in an Anjou village, trying to make it on watercolor sales and the tail end of some very slim savings. It was under those circumstances that I picked up the burnt onion gambit.

It was a dark and stormy night, just the right climate for necessity to give birth to a happy invention. I was cooking in my French fireplace at the time and the dish of the evening was going to be a tomato sauce over pasta. Waiting for my meager supply of onions to become golden, I reached for a hooker of local red to exercise my sipping elbow. The cheerful flames of the fire took my mind off what I was supposed to be doing just long enough for "golden" to become "charred." They smelled as good as I was beginning to feel. Since I didn't care to brave the elements on an onion-borrowing mission, I just went ahead and dumped in the tomatoes and peppers as planned. The result was serendipity.

From then on, I have often used burnt onions as a base for tomato-based sauces. Years later, when "no-name" items started showing up in U.S. supermarkets, I decided to suspend aversion to my ready-made stuff and picked up a quart of generic spaghetti sauce to experiment with during some future emergency. When the trencherpersons showed up by surprise last winter, our freezer looked like Mother Hubbard's and the guests were close to ravenous. I figured it was as good a time as any to carry out the test. . . .

Out came the giant iron frying pan and in went some oil and a couple of medium-sized onions sliced in thin rounds. I let them stay there until they turned black. These got a few raised eyebrows but I served a third round of California red and went on with the job. I added another sliced onion and a few cloves of mashed garlic, poured in the quart of store-bought sauce, added a can of puréed tomatoes, some oregano and red wine. Cooked on high heat with frequent stirring, the sauce soon thickened up to the right consistency and it brought raves all around.

Chemist friends have explained that the carbonization of the onions converts them to sugar. Whatever happens to them, charred onions are a powerful appetite stimulator. I can remember going to Havre de Grace when I was still at the age when hamburgers were considered regular food. Uncle Roy James owned a piece of the race-track there and to liven up his life during the racing season, he ran a hamburger stand at the edge of his property. Whenever business got too slack, he'd yell over to one of the short-order wizards: "Billy-Jo, throw a coupla onions on the grill—that'll bring 'em in . . ." And the longer the onions sizzled and slowly turned crisp, the more people who hadn't even realized that they were hungry got dragged in by their noses.

Incidentally, of all the magnificent things there are to eat in France, spaghetti is not one of them. And that goes double for Spain and Portugal. Their spaghetti is usually cooked to near mush and whatever sauce is used is added out in the kitchen, hours ahead of time. It's like stuff they served in the army or boarding school. Great spaghetti is done well only by Italians and some Americans, particularly those whose names end in vowels. The French feel very strongly about spaghetti and their negative reactions to it are pure chauvinism—probably because they didn't send Marco Polo to the Orient to discover it. As a result, they have not cultivated the technique of raising it above "palatable." (They do wonders with noodles, though—usually thanks to butter and mild cheese like Gruyère.) In fact, the rare times when a French driver is passed on the highway by a carefree speed-demon, the epithet *"Mangeurs de spaghetti!!"* (spaghetti-eaters) is often shouted automatically since a hot-blooded Italian is about the only tourist capable of and sufficiently foolhardy to cut past fast Frenchmen who are known to get pretty *rapide* hurrying home to a leisurely meal!

3 | seafood

While I was growing up in Pennsylvania, almost the only fish that ever came into our house were guppies and an occasional kipper. I was definitely underprivileged. I didn't realize what I was missing until I went to France for graduate work where I learned fish and French at the same time. I've become permanently hooked on both.

Recently in the U.S. the public has been subjected to a plethora of piscatorial praise urging one and all to eat more fish and live longer as a result. Unfortunately, pollution has gotten into the act and scientists have been telling us that fish is not always safe to consume. Fish has a lot of company sharing the bad-mouthing. Steroids and antibiotics show up in meat, chemical fertilizers in plants, cholesterol in nearly everything that tastes good. God knows what is in the water, and . . . the list is endless.

I intend to keep on eating what I like, exercising a modicum of restraint on certain comestibles. At the same time, I try not to worry that every bite I take is doing me more harm than good.

With this in mind, I'd like to begin my fishing line by telling you about some of the more exotic preparations I've enjoyed—exotic to us but everyday fare to some people somewhere. Let's start down in the Caribbean where fish is plentiful and relatively uncontaminated. There are fish-freaks who denigrate warm-water fish (i.e., tropical) for reasons of texture and blandness. If you share their doubts, ignore them for the moment. Try some of the ways they fix fish in the French Antilles—they taste good no matter where the fish comes from and are perfectly feasible up here in the north.

Eating seafood in the Caribbean involves a whole new kettle of fish. In an area where a large proportion of the daily diet comes from the ocean, native chefs have devised many different preparations to stave off boredom. Here are some of the methods they use that I don't think you'll find in your current kitchen bible. Take for example:

le vrai court-bouillon

Court-bouillon is French for a short simmering (literally, *short-boiling*). One uses a *court-bouillon* to poach fish and meat. It is basically composed of a lot of water, a little vinegar, white or red wine, whole peppercorns and a *bouquet garni.* You'll find lots of suggestions for using one in standard cook books. In principle, fish or meat is immersed in this liquid and boiled until done.

Such is not the *court-bouillon* we are dealing with here. According to cooks in the French Antilles, this is a misnomer and should be called a *long-bouillon*, because it takes so long and wastes much of the fish flavor in the broth. These Creole experts maintain that they have *le vrai court-bouillon* (the real court-bouillon) and even have a proverb to back it up: *Election sans fraude, cé cou-bouillon sans piment.* (An election without fraud is as dull as a court-bouillon without hot pepper). Their spelling is not what you are used to, but then Creole is not really a written language with strict rules. Neither is Creole cooking but it tastes good and is a fine change of pace for anyone seeking new flavor in life.

Actually, the short part of making a Creole *court-bouillon* means only the time it's on the fire. There is some marinating to be done and that takes a while. Begin by slicing up whatever fish you have on hand in pieces about big enough for one person. The fact that you can use just about any fair-sized fish makes this a good dish to try when a friend has gone fishing and comes home with a finny hodgepodge. Cover the slices with the juice of two lemons, a glass of dry white wine, salt, garlic and pepper. The pepper here is not that grey stuff called *poivre* that you tap out of a shaker but the red "hot" variety known as *"piment,"* which should be fresh if you can manage it. (I keep a small pepper tree in the kitchen for this and other delights like *"piri-piri,"* which I explain in another part of this book.)

Let the marinade work for at least an hour and while it's doing its stuff, mince some shallots and chives. Combine them with chopped-up tomatoes. This standard combination can be varied according to what you have on hand. Though shallots are readily available these days, they are expensive and onions or scallions will do nicely. Tomatoes are best when fresh, except for the styrofoam things we in the North have to use in winter. Those are better replaced by ones from a can.

When the tomatoes and onions have gotten time to become acquainted, put in the pieces of fish and cook until they too have become coated and slightly "seized." At this point, put in just enough hot water to cover the morsels and add half again as much dry white wine. Add a *bouquet garni* and hot pepper, well mashed in lemon juice. The amount of pepper you use depends on your threshold of heat tolerance. Go easy on it the first time you try this. You can always sprinkle on some *piri-piri* later if you're a real glutton for punishment, but once it's in there, you can't take it out.

Often in Creole cooking, the tomato-onion mixture is either reinforced or supplanted by *beurre rouge,* a mixture of lard, *rocou* and salt—lots of salt. *Rocou* is a Brazilian Indian word for the seed of a South American jungle tree of the same name. The only other place you are likely to experience it is in some Dutch cheeses which get their orange-red tint from it. In cheese, it comes in such small doses that you might not notice its taste. Chances are that you won't find *beurre rouge* at your local shop unless you live in an "ethnic" neighborhood, but if you do, watch out for its saltiness. The *beurre rouge* should be melted and divested of its salt crystals before becoming infused with the *court-bouillon.* It is awfully, awfully good. I didn't think to buy any of it when I was in the Caribbean the first time, but I was later richly rewarded by *Madame E. Claire* (that is her real name, so help me), who was working for PanAm at the time. She shipped me several tins when I mentioned my oversight to her in the departure lounge on Guadeloupe. Curiously, the product comes from Bordeaux and not the Caribbean!

Here comes the "short" part of the *court-bouillon,* because only a few minutes are needed to complete the wonder. I remove the fish while it's still firm—it is done enough when it has lost its translucency. Then, for a few more minutes on high flame, I reduce the remaining bouillon from watery to smooth and pour it over the fish. You can serve it in a large bowl for everyone to pick from or in individual soup plates. The latter way will make sure the nifty sauce won't be wasted. The ideal accompaniment is plain boiled rice. See "Nicerice" under vegetables.

You will want plenty to drink with this dish and I suggest a light, dry, not very fancy white or chilled red. Preceded by *crudités,* followed by *bananes flambées, court-bouillon antillais* will give you a taste of the tropics. All you need to do is turn on your sun lamp, drag out the potted palm (an aspidistra will do), sprinkle some sand on the floor and you won't even have to leave home to go native.

blaff de poissons

Blaff, a.k.a. *blafe,* is much more like a non-tropical court-bouillon. Its main characteristic is that it is hotter than a fireman's kneecap protector—*piment* is there in full splendor. In effect, it is a true bouillon with large pieces of fish swimming in it. It is found more often in Martinique and French Guiana than it is in Guadeloupe, but even the latter isle will offer you plenty of chances to sample it unless you want to beat them to it and try it out at home.

To make your own *blaff*, cut up and marinate fish just as you would for the *court-bouillon antillais*. In a different large pot, put about a half pint of water and dry white wine for each pound of fish. (Half and half is about right and you can use jug wine.) Add the juice of half of one of our lemons (tropical ones are smaller and taste a little like limes but could also be used here), a large clove or two small ones, 2 cloves of garlic (crushed), pepper, a small onion and a dash of fennel if you like it. (These amounts are per pound of fish, more or less.) Toss in a *bouquet garni* and some parsley (now and/or later) and you're in business. Let this creation boil half an hour or so, until it has a pronounced flavor. Then, add the fish for at least another 10 minutes of boiling. Remove the solid condiments like the cloves and the *bouquet* and serve the fish in bowls. Cover it with the bouillon and the onions and parsley used in cooking. Serve with plenty of rice.

Experts pretend that to qualify as authentic, a *blaff* bouillon should include *Bois d'Inde*. This is also known as Jamaican pepper, which in turn goes under aliases including one designating the seeds of an aromatic bay tree. After a lot of searching around back home for the spice by its exotic names, I finally found out that it was good old allspice all along. This is a ground-up berry which tastes like cloves, nutmeg and cinnamon. In the past, I had assumed that it was a manufactured mixture and it wasn't until I saw it growing in Hawaii that I realized that allspice is the fruit of a single tree! I have since found that it does a lot for fish whether I'm cooking tropical or Yankee.

Intrigued by the word *blaff*, I went to some pains to find out where it came from. I discovered that theories vary but a quite reasonable one comes out of Dutch Guiana. There's a term there, *braf*, which stands for somewhat eclectic cooking methods in which practically anything goes. For example, you could lace salt pork with boiled iguana, if that's your bag, and call it *braf*. I think I might be inclined to juxtapose the center letters and make it "barf," but I sometimes find the left hemisphere of my brain hard to compromise.

At any rate, *braf* suited the Creoles as a designation for some of their more exotic culinary efforts. However, not unlike certain Orientals, they have a rough time reeling off "r's" so they have settled for *blaff*. Incidentally, the natives of the off-islands of Guadeloupe don't go for iguana as do certain other Caribbean people, although they have nothing against the idea. The French can cook just about anything into edibility. The problem comes with a logical apprehension concerning the steady diet of the local iguanas who delight in gorging themselves on the *mancenillier* (manchineel in English). This is a bush-like tree which thrives in that area. The *mancellinier* has toxic greenery which will bruise your skin if you brush up against it and can kill you if you eat it. Iguanas may not look very smart but they are survivors!

try a dab of *daube*

One more tropical fish tale which works well at home is *daube de poisson*. *Daube* actually stands for stewing of sorts in French, but the Creoles in adopting the word have made a few changes. When applied to fish, *daube* works this way:

Once again the fish is cut into fairly large pieces that will look like those swordfish steaks that go for around eight dollars a pound. Big fish, like tuna and medium-sized shark, are good for this method. It should first be marinated just as though you were going to make a *court-bouillon antillais* or a *blaff*. Then flour the fish and pop it into a hot frying pan with a bit of bubbling oil. When the fish is about half done, remove it from the pan. Add a bit more oil and/or butter, some finely minced onions and a few chives, salt, pepper and a bit of thyme. As soon as the onions begin to blush, place the fish on top of them, put in a small amount of hot water and keep heating while you check for taste, to decide whether or not more seasoning is required. Then cover, cook for ten minutes, peeking from time to time to make sure that it won't get dry or overcooked. Just before you call the troops to table, add some capers and lemon juice and prepare for a treat.

If you have fish big enough for this dish, there is nothing that says you can't cook them over the grill instead. It wouldn't be *daube* anymore, but *poissons grillés* are mighty tasty when introduced to charcoal or wood fires *after* marinating.

tips from the cod father

Even though we didn't get fish at home, I cannot say that I wasn't exposed to it at all as a kid. After all, I did eat at school and, once in a great while, wound up in a diner, the closest thing we had to a fast-food outlet in the olden days. Diners ranged from miserable to great and still do when you find the rare ones still around. A consistent item on diner menus, back then, was codfish cakes which, as I recall, were not among my top ten treats. School versions didn't raise them in my esteem either. I probably would not have cared for *acras* either, at that stage in life. But now I dig them and before we leave the Caribbean for the time being, let's have a look at *their* codfish fritters which are called *acras*.

Since so much cod is still salted for preservation and export, it will be found in some of its more succulent dishes overseas. The Caribbean, for example, gets salt cod, which seems strange since they have so many other fish practically leaping out of the sea to be consumed.

Actually, the presence of salt cod down there is a hangover from slavery days. Early New Englanders set sail for Europe to sell codfish, mostly to the Portuguese and Spanish. With the income, they bought African slaves and fed them on the way across the Atlantic with cod that they hadn't sold. With slave money, they filled up their ships with molasses and sugar in the Caribbean and brought those products back to New England distilleries and grocers to complete the circle. There are still many living from those fortunes today, but the West Indians' main inheritance from this traffic is their persistent predilection for cod.

The tropical area that I am most familiar with is the French Antilles, where they make a first course called "*acras*," rather wild Caribbean cod cakes. *Acra* is a word meaning vegetable fritter in the parts of Africa whence came slaves to the Antilles. Tropical vegetables make great *acras* but we are concerned with the cod right now so I shall give you a rundown on how "*acras de morue*" are made. I have consumed many times my weight in these tasty morsels which quite often I helped to prepare, at least with my eyes. Here's a rough idea of how to prepare them.

Desalt some dried cod in several changes of cold water. Put the pieces of cod on some sort of rack so that the underside of the fish won't be touching the receptacle used for soaking. Cover them over with fresh water for 6 or 7 hours, dump the water and do it again. Two or three changes of water should get enough of the salt out.

To a quarter pound of fish add one hot pepper, a scattering of scallions, chives if you've got 'em, a clove of garlic, some parsley and thyme. You'll want to chop these ingredients up as fine as you can before they are mixed with the fish. In the absence of a mortar, I use a wooden chopping bowl. While all these fine tastes are mingling, make a batter from a cup of flour, 3 ounces of butter, a half cup of milk and 2 beaten eggs. Whomp all this together and let it rest 3 or 4 hours. Mix the batter and the fish and you are all set. When you are ready to start eating, drop spoonfuls of the mixture into hot oil—deep if possible. As soon as they are slightly golden, they are ready. If you don't shoo everyone out of the kitchen, you'll never make it to the table with a full plate of *acras*—which may be just as well anyway since they should be eaten hot.

on first looking into french cod

Even though I've lived on Cape Cod for many years, I never really appreciated the local specialty until I began sampling tropical and European versions of fish. Long before I learned about *Blaffs* and *Acras*, I enjoyed my first ethereal cod experience when I lived with a devout French family who frequently on Friday served a dish called *Brandade de Morue*. This is a preparation native to the *Languedoc*, the Mediterranean part of southern France between Provence and the Pyrenees. As a student and eventually teacher thereabouts, I came to know and appreciate *Brandade de Morue* in a big way.

Où est le chef?

FRENCH COD

Brandade is from an old Provençal word, *branda*, which means simply "stirred up" and *morue* is French for codfish and, on occasion, lady of very-easy virtue.

Since cod is native to the U.S., it has traditionally arrived in Europe as dried, salted fish. Where I live cod is available just as it is when it leaves the nets. But since there are so many recipes based on the dried version, much of the world has developed ways to prepare it in its non-fresh form. More's the pity because fresh cod is tough to beat. Be that as it may, here's a French specialty you may enjoy far from the sea.

brandade de morue

Brandade calls for dried codfish which always requires some advance preparation and elbow grease. The first goal is to soak out the salt which we checked out while making *Acras*. When the salt is gone, poach the cod in plain water for about 8 minutes, being very careful TO KEEP IT FROM BOILING.

While the simmering is going on, crush a pair of garlic cloves in a roomy bowl. A mortar would make it authentic but not too many of us have mortars at hand these days. On the other hand, a food processor is absolutely perfect for making this preparation.

If you work by hand, flake and add the cod, crushing it along with the garlic. For one pound of fish, dribble in about half a pint of fragrant olive oil. Go slowly, incorporating the oil as you go along, the way you would make a mayonnaise. It takes effort but it's worth it. With a processor, just dump in everything and let 'er rip.

When you have a snow white unctuous mass, put it in a pan over very low heat and while stirring continuously, add a little over two ounces of sour cream. (The French use *crème fraîche*, which is not as sour as sour cream but not as sweet as our fresh cream.) You'll eventually wind up with something the consistency of sticky mashed potatoes. All you need add is a dash of lemon juice, some ground pepper and some salt—if there's none left in the fish—BUT TASTE FIRST TO MAKE SURE.

Some like it hot, and some like it cold. If you want to serve this hot, heat it enough to suit yourself and serve it with boiled potatoes and a green salad. If you prefer it cold, take it off the fire when the cream is well mixed in and let it cool. Cold boiled potatoes with vinaigrette make a good match. I like it both ways.

If you get hooked on *brandade de morue*, you might want to try it in an omelet. Simply beat up the requisite number of eggs, make an omelet after your fashion and just before it gets too done, drop a big blob of *brandade* in the middle. Fold over the sides and watch the shy eaters come back for seconds.

gold-plated cod

It was when I moved to Portugal, that I realized there was an entire national cuisine based on the cod. They say that the Portuguese have a different cod recipe for every day in the year, and I wouldn't be surprised if there weren't a few more lurking in the Portuguese outback for leap years.

Here is a version I first met at a luncheon given by the aunt of a young Portuguese lady of distinguished lineage—the bride-to-be of an American friend of ours who directed the Portuguese branch of Mobil at the time. The bride's aunt is a *marquesa* and she lives in a beautiful pink palace. She had opened one of the larger dining-rooms for the pre-nuptial meal.

To give you an idea of the surroundings, there was an El Greco peering down from the wall of an adjacent den. The dining table, just a bit shorter than a soccer field, was laden with gold plates and utensils. Since much of my previous snacking in Portugal had taken place in lean-tos, I was delighted to deal with pure opulence for a change. Raw cod would probably have been o.k. under the circumstances, but the dish of the day, *bacalhau d'oiro*, cod of gold, definitely fit the scene.

Golden codfish is as beautiful to look at and savor as it is easy to prepare. It even tastes good on plain old plates and if you want to try your hand at it, here's what to do:

Soak the cod in several changes of water until most of the salt is gone. Then pull it apart into strips like fat short shoelaces. That's the boring part. From there on, it's downhill. Cut a couple of onions into thin rings and then slice them so that they resemble the form of the cod strips. Slowly turn the onions golden in olive oil over low heat. Toss in the cod and heat the mixture without stirring too much in order not to spoil the strands. While the cod and onions are taking on heat, fry some shoestring potatoes—either in a frying pan or deep fat. Just before you are ready to serve the dish, add two slightly beaten eggs to the already warmed fish. As soon as the eggs begin to thicken, put in the shoestring potatoes and stir together gently. Serve at once!

A CAPE COD COD

cape cod cod

There is plenty of fresh cod on the Cape these days. It's often haddock or
scrod, the latter being the young of cod or haddock, which are not exactly
the same but close enough for confusion (and good enough for off-color jokes
about little old ladies on their way to Boston for dinner). Some restaurants list
it as "schrod," which means that it will cost more and/or the chef may not
know any more about spelling than he does about cooking. Knowledgeable
Bostonians maintain that the excess "h" indicates to restaurant patrons that
the schrod of the day is actually haddock rather than young cod. There are
other versions of how the "h" got into the act. This one seems about the
most logical to me so I'll get the "h" out of this argument.

Whichever kind is used, much of the fish in New England is more notable
for its freshness and natural good taste than its method of preparation. Even
though there are legions of good fish cooks in the area, they do their best
dishes *at home*. Out in restaurant and fish-shack land, it's "fillet and fry" and
shovel on the French fries and cole slaw. Pre-frozen fries and utterly
unimaginative slaw have a tendency to stifle one's eating pleasure in the fast-
fish-lane. To enjoy *commercially prepared* fish at its best, one has to look
elsewhere. There's hope on the horizon, however. "Non-native" restaurants
have been springing up lately and they have gone a long way toward
glamorizing the eating-out scene. As a rule, though, you cannot count on
very exciting *commercial* cuisine dishes in a region where many "natives"
still settle for traditional treats such as boiled dinners and beans drenched in
molasses.

If you're lucky, though, you might get invited out for some "Cape Cod
Turkey." That's de-salted, salted cod, poached and served on toast with a
cream sauce and slices of hard-boiled eggs. It's a good fill-in for those cold
winter days when the fishermen leave the "big" drink for a lot of small ones
at home.

NOTE: For anyone wondering why I have placed such emphasis on salted
cod—rest assured that *fresh* cod is a fantastic fish that should be enjoyed

whenever possible. The hitch is that I can get it fresh just about any time of the year, even if I have to catch it myself. You might not be able to. But you can get the dried version almost anywhere, anytime.

Fresh and dried have such different tastes that when eating them, it would be easy to assume that they were two different fish. Dried cod has a lot of flavor that has to be complemented or overcome. Fresh cod is delicate and amenable to all sorts of subtle sauces or just plain butter. The end results are distinctly different, and both are good eating. I just wanted to make sure that you could read about the one you are sure to be able to enjoy if the spirit moves you.

squid is better than it sounds

One of my fondest memories of Portugal is watching the *lula* boats bob up and down like floating strings of diamonds on the night sea. From my upstairs porch, I could watch them most of the year and *lulas* became then (and still are) a favorite dish of mine. I see plenty of them here on Cape Cod but they are more likely to wind up on the end of a fish-hook than in a frying pan.

Americans have a tendency to draw the line at *lulas* as a comestible item. They won't know what they are missing until they try them. You might not either, if I don't mention now that *lula* is Portuguese for squid. It's a fanciful name but not so common here in the U.S. as some form of *calamar* or *calamari*, which you will bump into occasionally in Spanish and Italian restaurants. I'm happy to say that they are appearing more and more frequently in our supermarkets, labelled prosaically "squid." They come frozen or fresh, cleaned or just as they came out of the water. Fresh and untampered with are far and away the best.

A delightful way to glide into the pleasures of *lula* consumption is via the French fried route. In fact, if you are not really paying close attention, you could easily mistake the looks of a fried *lula* for those of a French fried onion ring. They look much alike and they are both delicious—but quite different to the taste if the frying-oil is fresh. The next time you go for some deep-sea fishing bait, get a big package of squid from the supermarket and put some aside for the kitchen. That way, if the finny friends are not biting, you will be when you get back home.

Clean the *lulas* under running water and remove everything you can until you are left with little white sacs. The heads and tentacles are good too, but they are better used in other recipes. If you are trying to break in skeptics, stick with French-frying for starters. Slice the sacs in rings with a very sharp knife. For the tastiest and tenderest treats, salt and pepper the little circles and let them sit in lemon juice for a couple of hours. Then dip them in flour and wave them through a beaten egg on their way to the fryer. They have a tendency to spit and pop in the hot oil so watch your eyes. Twenty to thirty

seconds should be enough. Serve with lemon wedges. Once you try them—
if they are done properly and don't turn out like bicycle tire patches from
overcooking—you'll find it hard to quit eating them.

lulas & rice are very nice!

If you are not keen on deep frying, clean and cut the *lulas* the same way
and do them up with garlic, an onion or two, hot pepper flakes and some
paprika (*colorau* if you can find it). See page 4. Braise onions briefly and
then simmer everything together in olive oil. Keep the combination moist
with white wine and put on a kettle for some rice. By the time the rice is
ready, the *lulas* will be too. All you have to do is toss some sherry into the
pan at the last minute, turn up the heat to de-alcoholize the sherry, but be
quick about it lest the wine flavor evaporate. Put little volcanoes of rice in
bowls and fill up the craters with the *lulas*. With rough red wine and salad,
you've got yourself a treat.

There are many other ways to prepare *lulas* and once you get over the idea
that you don't want to eat squid, which is why I keep calling them *lulas*, you
will be on your way to good eating. They are supposed to be quite restorative
and those into venery will appreciate them.

When I lived in Portugal, much of the food-buying was done by Ilda, the lady who did for me. Whenever she went off to lay in a supply of *lulas* at the fish market, it was sure to produce a chorus of guffaws. She would be asked if her husband were falling down on the job and when she would reply that he wasn't and that the *lulas* were for her boss, it would get a second, heartier round of laughs. As a result, she switched to buying our *lulas* from the motorcycle fish-monger who putted by the house every morning. In spite of being from inland (one of the reasons she was open to teasing by the coastal folk), she had a good hand with the *lulas*. I'll give you just two more suggestions for different preparations she whipped up.

When cleaning the little critters, you will notice that the sacs lend themselves quite readily to stuffing. With this in mind, clean some carefully so as not to put holes in them and prepare a stuffing like this: chop up the heads and tentacles beyond recognition and put them in bread crumbs with a little milk to hold things together. Cook very small pieces of salt pork (or bacon) and *linguiça* together with a minced onion in a bit of olive oil. When the onion gets golden, put in the bread crumb ensemble, a little bit of salt, some grated nutmeg and a beaten egg. Mix together thoroughly and stuff the *lulas*. Leave a little room for expansion so you don't wind up with a ceiling full of *lula* stuffing, and close the ends with toothpicks. The kids will probably love to help you with this (the stuffing that is).

I'm so used to Iberian sausages that I tend to lose sight of the fact that not everybody knows about them. That word *linguiça* that whizzed by is a case in point. It and a companion *chouriço* are fairly common in much of New England but might need explanation for those in other regions whose settlers sprang from different roots. *Linguiça* and *chouriço* are almost interchangeable in the U.S. In Portugal, *linguiça* is generally made of pork and, unlike the U.S. variety, is dark to black. Their Spanish cousin, *chorizo*, is red to orange in color and goes from hot and spicy up in Basque country to milder versions down in Andalusia—a switch on the usual hotter-in-the-south condition for food in general. The versions of these sausages made in the U.S. are often quite good but they are not the same as you would get in the old country.

Now for the cooking—chop up a large onion and begin to cook it in a bit of olive oil. When the pieces become translucent, add 4 ground tomatoes or a medium-sized can of them if they are not in season, some *piri-piri* and a cup of white wine. Put in the *lulas*, which are now *recheadas* (stuffed) and cook over moderate heat. The time this takes depends mainly on the size of the *lulas*; you'll have to use your own judgment. Add water if the dish starts getting too dry.

Lulas have cousins called *chocos* (cuttlefish), which, as far as cuisine is concerned, are treated the same. Both have backbones, however, which should be removed before cooking. The backbones are those thin, white, oblong porous bones used by caged canaries to hone their beaks. Cuttlefish are affectionate little creatures and it's their urge for togetherness that sometimes spells their undoing. Portuguese striplings catch girl cuttlefish (*chocas*) with hooks and then lead them around on a string in shallow waters. If a boy cuttlefish (*choco*) gets in the neighborhood, the *choca* blushes. That's how the kids, and the *chocos*, can tell which is which. When the *choco* sees the potential love of his life floating leisurely by, he wiggles over to cuddle and—zap!—he gets harpooned right in the kisser and it's off to the *caldeirada* for him.

A *caldeirada* is the contents of a *caldeira*, which is Portuguese for cauldron. It is also what they call a fish stew most of the time, whatever it is cooked in. (The word "chowder" comes from the same roots.) Here's a *caldeirada de lulas* which uses a pressure cooker. This is not only fast but helps take some of the springiness out of adult *lulas*.

Slice carefully cleaned *lulas* into hoops again and potatoes in quarters— two pounds of each will get you off to a good start. Slice two medium onions and turn them golden in olive oil. Put in the *lulas*. (Heads, etc., are optional, but perhaps the *lulas* are more attractive without them.) When the *lulas* begin to lose their pale look, add two tablespoons of some sort of fat, salt pork, vegetable shortening or even more oil. Add salt, paprika, 3 or 4 tomatoes cut up, a bay leaf, a sprig of parsley, some grated nutmeg, half a cup of white wine and a jigger of vinegar. Batten down the cover on the cooker, and let the pressure come up to valve-jiggling level. Leave it that way for 5 minutes, take off the stove and cool the cooker quickly in water. It's like being able to leave a rich tomato sauce bubbling away at the back of the stove for several hours! Try this with boiled rice and keep the *piri-piri* handy.

just plain fish

Such esoteric fare as *blaff* and *lulas* are fun to read about but maybe you're more tuned in to eating plainer fare. If so, hang on. I used to be intimidated by the thought of cooking fish. For some reason, I didn't expect to be able to make it palatable. This was doubtless because my land-locked youth provided next to no fish experience. I've been making up for this ever since. After cutting my teeth on fancy foreign fish dishes and learning how to prepare them, I finally got around to simpler preparations. I found that cooking fish straightforwardly is simple and fast. If we start out with good, fresh fish, the results will be good too. The two main pitfalls are overcooking and picking a method not suitable to a given fish.

There are oily fish like mackerel, tuna and bluefish. These lend themselves to baking or grilling. This type has plenty of taste, and if it is to be perked up more, you have to let yourself go to town on the seasoning.

If you are into charcoal broiling, grilled bluefish is hard to beat. I cut slashes along the sides and insert slivers of garlic. There's enough flavor (and oil) in the fish so that all you have to do is plop it on the grill, turning it over once when the bottom half is done. If you are the slightest bit apprehensive about pollution, discard the skin and the dark meat which is where most of the uninvited chemicals reside.

SARDINE

The following short interlude is a suggestion for real grilled-fish fans to keep in mind if they happen to get to Europe where they can sample sardines whose length can be measured in double-digit inches!

Fresh sardines are to tinned ones something like fresh cod is to dried—that is, they taste different but are equally delicious. Although I have seen fresh sardines in our markets, they do not show up often. They are among my favorite grilled fish. I don't mean those little ones from cans but the kind they eat all over Portugal and Spain, among other places. That's a little far to go for lunch but if ever you are over there, be sure to give them a try. There's no mistaking where they are available. Your nose will pick up their distinctive aroma long before you lay eyes on the place where they are cooking. In fact, when I am hungry in a strange town in Portugal, I use the sardine sniffing method to ferret out a good spot to eat. More often than not, when there are sardines on the grill, there are partridges in the oven (or on *another* grill).

To give Spain equal billing, I hasten to point out the grilled sardine capital of the known universe, which is Santurce, a suburb of Bilbao up in Basque country. There, you will find lots of plain, rough tables, each long enough to seat a scout troop and crowded with hungry Spaniards yelling for more sardines. And I'm talking real sardines here, some of them close to a foot long. Wine and beer flow by the pitcher and, for non-fin fans, there are chicken and meat roasting too.

Meanwhile, back in the kitchen at home: When you want to cook oily fish in the oven, use a large baking dish and surround the fish with mushrooms, tomatoes, green peppers and onions—pour on some dry white wine and herbs of your choice. Shove into a hot (400–450 degree) oven. The length of time for baking is roughly 10 minutes to the inch. This inch is the thickness of the piece of fish at its thickest. If you measured lengthwise, even the cat wouldn't touch the results. Start timing when the wine bubbles. If you have a large fish, don't put the vegetables in until the last ten minutes.

Actually, when I prepare fish this way, I put the onions in first and heat them in a bit of butter or oil until they go limp. Then the fish goes on top. I also add garlic to the vegetables but I'm well aware that not everyone shares my fondness for it.

If you don't want to mess around with all the vegetables, here's an easy out. Cover your fish (on both sides) with mayonnaise and sprinkle it with herbs of your choice. Bake it in a hot oven at 10 minutes to the inch. Try it; you'll like it. Some go as far as to add breadcrumbs or — gulp — cornmeal. (The latter, for me at any rate, is more at home with an occasional fried clam. In the fish department, it should be reserved for a fresh-water creature like trout, cooked over a campfire way out in the woods.)

These oily fish will still be recognizable by flavor after they're done in either of these two ways. For that matter, you can pan-fry them too, but I find that they have more taste than I care for when done that way.

Delicate fish, like flounder, perch and sole, however, are quite tasty when pan-fried. Melt butter to bubbling stage, throw in fish, add seasonings if you wish and turn once. Use a pan large enough so that there will be room between the pieces. The oily fish routine for these milder specimens would be a bit silly. Chances are you wouldn't know what you're eating.

When you have more time to spare, there are many delicious (and more complicated) ways to prepare more subtly flavored fish. There are purists who resist embellishing them with wine and herbs. They don't know what they're missing. Rather than repeat a bunch of recipes you can find in books devoted to the subject, I'll simply offer a suggestion worth its weight in fillets: "DON'T OVERCOOK." Be very careful about cooking "until the fish *flakes*." Most of the time when it gets to this stage, it's overdone.

fish that swim through the door

One of the blessing of living by the sea is that occasionally "fish swim through the door." Hurricanes aside, this is a local expression describing the happy moment when friends show up with their latest catch. Just how good friends they are can be determined by the quality and, more important, the state of the fish, i.e., cleaned or *au naturel*. My favorite gourmet fish chef has quite an eye for those clever with the hook and net. She allows as how she knows when "their" relationship dwindles to merely Platonic when the fish get dumped in her sink as they arrived from the depths. She's pretty clever too, and usually manages to persuade the donor that catching is not enough if she is expected to transform the beauties into comestibility. Fish and fisherpersons are relegated to the out-of-doors to perform the necessary cosmetology while she gets ready for her part of the act. When confronted with a large variety, this is how she goes about the affair:

In a large pot, she softens a few sliced onions in hot olive oil. When the onions turn transparent, she squeezes in a few cloves of garlic. By this time, she expects a few fish heads and bones, which she rinses and throws in the pot. White wine and water follow, about half and half, and possibly a few shooters of bottled clam juice if she has it on hand. Herbs and spices are next. They are a matter of taste but hers calls for basil, thyme, a generous pinch of fennel seed, at least one bay leaf and several turns of the pepper mill. Much to my liking, she also adds red pepper, dried or fresh, and, as a kicker, a few inches of orange peel, also dried or fresh. No salt is necessary or called for.

This fragrant elixir is left to simmer while she cuts the fish into bite-sized morsels. Uniformity in these small sizes sees to it that the different qualities of fish get done at about the same time. She leaves out the heavy duty fish like mackerel and blues which would overpower the blend.

When the exciting aroma has everyone chomping at the bit, it's time to strain out the bones and various flotsam which are ready to discard. If she is lucky enough to be doing this during tomato season, she adds half a dozen fresh ones, preferably without skin, pulp and seeds. Out of season, she adds a jar or two of re-bought spaghetti sauce (meatless) which anyone, sound of mind, would find superior to winter freight-ripened pink lumps masquerading as the real things. If necessary, add a bit more water—the idea is to have about a pint of broth per eater.

At last, in go the fish. She simmers them until all the pieces are opaque which, if they were properly sized, happens all at once. When there are mussels and/or clams about—crustaceans too, if you're lucky—they go in (thoroughly scrubbed) with the fish. It's about a photo finish for them to open up, done, just as the fish are at perfection. (At the last minute or two, you can even add some thin *lula* rings.)

How you present this at the table depends largely on how long you can restrain the company from diving into the pot. Ideally, arrange the fish over toasted bread, deploy any shellfish about the individual bowls or plates, and ladle on the broth. Chopped parsley and lemon wedges go nicely with the ensemble. If there is anything left in the pot, keep it warm but DON'T let the fish cook any more.

PS If you can't handle heads and bones to make a fish stock, substitute additional clam juice. You'll be missing something but it won't be a case of nerves over skeletons.

PPS If you cannot wait to get to the seashore to give this concoction a whirl, you can make quite an acceptable version with frozen fish too. So live it up, wherever you are.

beurre blanc

There's no mistaking the principal ingredient of the last recipe. To be fair to all, I must mention the other end of the fish scale for those who don't really care for fish but indulge occasionally to humor the rest of us. Actually, this is about a sauce. It is so good that cardboard cod covered with it would be comestible. It's *beurre blanc* (white butter) and almost all food writers seem to get carried away with it these days. Some of their versions might upset persnickety French who have a traditional way of making it and are equally hidebound about what they serve it with, namely, shad or pike (*alose or brochet*).

These days, even the French are bending the rules about what goes with what. Whatever, I'm giving you the inside dope on a real thing, as I first encountered it back in the '50's! Even those who don't as a rule appreciate fish will go bananas if you cover the offering with *beurre blanc*.

Beurre blanc is native to the upper western part of France where it is frequently called *Beurre Blanc Nantais* after Nantes, the principal city of the Loire-Inférieure. It goes best with fresh water fish whose delicate flavor is raised to sheer luxury by this rich concoction. Making *beurre blanc* is simple but tricky. Once you get the hang of it, it's easier to make than hollandaise. It's much more special too, since not everyone who cooks is trying to imitate it (yet), the way they strive for a perfect Hollandaise.

Near where I lived in Anjou, there was a very informal, homey restaurant in St. Aubin. It was run by Madame Vigneron and a few of her many daughters, one of whom was walleyed, which made ordering a bit distracting. Madame was about 4 foot 2 inches (in both directions) and obviously did not shy away from her own cooking. She turned out some mighty fancy food and it was thanks to her that I learned the ropes on *beurre blanc*.

When the youngsters in my village (Chanzeaux) were feeling up to a treat, they gathered all the *escargots* for hundreds of meters around and persuaded me to take them over for lunch *chez* Madame. Since snails were another specialty of the house, they could usually work out a good barter arrangement. The kids filled up on *bife-frites* (steak and french fries) while I would opt for the *beurre blanc* with shad. It wasn't that they didn't care for snails, it's just that—like kids anywhere—they preferred *real* fast food. They also got an enormous kick out of the strabismic waitress who kept them in stitches no matter what they were eating.

I usually slipped out to the kitchen at some point on every visit to Madame Vigneron's and here's what I learned by repeatedly watching her prepare the delicacy in question:

The ingredients for *beurre blanc* are shallots, vinegar and butter—LOADS of butter, about half a pound of it per pound of fish! Your arteries won't thank you for getting hooked on *beurre blanc* but your taste buds will.

Mince a small handful of peeled shallots and put them in a saucepan with a quarter to half a cup of white vinegar. (Some include chopped parsley, but I prefer that as a garnish later on at serving time.) Heat the shallots, stirring them around, until they disintegrate to mush. If they start to get dry, add some more vinegar. The butter, which you should allow to get warm but not melted, is then added a chunk at a time, letting each one melt before adding another, until it is all incorporated and thoroughly heated up.

It is at this point that most cooks fail. Too much heat will turn the butter to oil and not enough will not allow the sauce to become as firm as it should be, a lot like a successful mayonnaise. It was by watching Madame Vigneon like a hawk that I learned the following gimmick which shaves chances of failure to a minimum. I'll bet that even Julia Child doesn't know about it and, if she does, she's been keeping it to herself. When you've finished adding all the butter, allow the pan to come to a bubble, NOT boil, and remove it immediately from the flame for a few moments. Do this three times in all and you should have a bang-up *beurre blanc*. This sauce is designed for poached fish, but if you want an even milder vehicle, try steaming.

steamed fish

You do not have to be an invalid to enjoy steamed fish. Not only can it be delicious but it has the further advantage of easy preparation by MICROWAVE! This is probably the simplest, fastest most painless possible way to get fish from the fridge to the table. Put thin filets of something like whitefish or fresh cod in a shallow baking dish. Pour in a little dry white wine, cover the fish with very thin slices of lemon and sprinkle on some chopped parsley. Cover the ensemble with Saranwrap or the equivalent and pop this into the microwave for a very short time. As a rule of thumb, the microwave generally takes about a third of the time that a regular hot oven would. Experience with your equipment will be the best guide. Err on the short side, however — you want the fish steamed, not vulcanized.

No micro? — no problem! Use a steamer just as you would for vegetables. Put the fish in a bowl of sorts, not directly over a colander, and steam away. Check after 10 minutes or so, depending on thickness of filets. If you don't plan to indulge in *beurre blanc* or a fancy sauce, it won't hurt to flavor up the fish with pepper and possibly some onion flakes and/or herbs. Dill is great for this.

If you prefer not to fool with the *beurre blanc*, have your steamed fish cold, with garlic mayonnaise. It's terrific on a steamy summer day.

Oily fish is not successful when steamed. A notable exception to this is salmon, which is hard to wreck no matter what you do to it.

the devil made me do this

To taper off with a grand fish finale, here's one more sauce suggestion: *à la Diable*, devil fashion. As I was winding up the fish section, salmon went on sale at under $3.00 per pound, an infrequent occurrence in these parts. I opted for steaks and cut a couple-of-pound piece into slices about ¾ of an inch thick. Under optimum conditions, I would have done them over charcoal, but it was raining so I went for something easier in order to stay in the kitchen. Thanks to my turbo-oven (see pastry), I could broil them with ease. All I had to do was sprinkle a little oil on both sides, grind on some pepper and spread the oil and pepper around to cover the steaks. The reason I say with ease is because the nature of the turbo-oven is that one is not required to flip whatever one is broiling in mid-stream. That's no problem with meat, but more delicately structured fish has a habit of falling to pieces when tampered with, especially if it's sliced very thin.

During the 8 minutes while the fish was broiling, I prepared the devil sauce. I softened up a stick (4 oz.) of butter and added the juice of half a big lemon, 2 tablespoons of strong mustard, a couple of tablespoons of fresh chopped chives, ditto for parsley. Then I added a generous amount of hot red pepper. The amount of pepper depends on your liking for same but obviously you wouldn't want so much that you couldn't make out the other flavors. I put the hot broiled salmon steaks on individual plates and divided up the "devil" equally over each one. My bottomless-pit nephew could have gone for another round.

Lacking a turbo-oven, here's another approach. Use an oven-proof frying pan and, while the oven is pre-heating on broil, do the steaks over lightly in the pan on high heat before they have a chance to become fragile. When they start to cook through, slosh in a puddle of white wine and transfer the pan to the broiler. Anywhere from 5 to 10 minutes should do it. Of course you can use other fish with this sauce, so don't wait for salmon to go on sale to try this out.

4 | meat and garlic

As you can see, I write about things I enjoy eating. This book is not the result of bunny-hunting through a batch of cookbooks in search of appealing recipes. Rather it is to tell you about personal experiences. You can enjoy many of them too without leaving home. I hope that you will.

Meat plays a large part in our national diet and the meat dishes that follow are all ones that I have been able to prepare here in the U.S. I don't deal with veal. I like it but I've found that American veal can't compare to American beef. In fact lamb and veal are both so much better in many other parts of the world that I don't bother with them unless I'm traveling. Top quality (i.e. expensive) roast beef and steak practically cook themselves with little or no added flavoring. So what I am going to tell you about involves more economical meat and chicken dishes.

From the looks of things, they all use garlic. In some preparations, it jumps out at the eater—in others, you might not even know that it's there. So, don't be put off if I call this section Meat and Garlic because you might be missing out on some real treats. For balance, I shall put in a piece about Virginia Ham. I can't remember when we haven't had one on hand and heartily suggest the custom for anyone who wants a real treat at a moment's notice.

Although the trend is changing, there are still many people who are almost proud of not cooking. The ultimate cop-out used is "I don't really have the time." Well, here's a main course that can be prepared in less time than it takes to thaw out a T.V. dinner.

When I get the chance, I head for the Caribbean any time of the year. It's an area not renowned for great food except for the French islands, which have a cuisine that takes advantage of French suavity combined with tropical spice. One evening when visiting some friends in Guadeloupe, I took along a kilo of beef instead of flowers. Since flowers practically grow out of the woodwork down there, *bifteck* makes a more welcome guest present. Caribbean *bifteck* will never be mistaken for an Omaha special, but by the time a French cook gets through with local beef, most of us won't be worrying about bovine ancestry.

bifteck à l'hélène

My hostess, Hélène, works all day to support her little family and as a consequence doesn't have much time to waste in the kitchen. What she turns out is usually fast and always superb. This is the way she fixed the gift-steer.

On a metal platter, she piled up about a head of garlic, carefully minced, a large lump of butter, plenty of ground pepper and a mound of chopped parsley. She bathed the lot with the juice of Caribbean lemons. (Guadeloupe lemons are the size of limes, the color of lemons, and taste somewhere between the two.)

Being at tropical temperature, the butter began to melt on its own while the cooking went on. (In the more temperate areas of the U.S., we might introduce the platter to some mild heat, not enough to cook the garlic because in this recipe it has to remain raw to be well done.) The beef was sliced into very thin pieces and quickly cooked in a frying pan. They haven't found out much about olive oil in that part of the tropics so their custom is to use regular cooking oil and sometimes a bit of butter for the meat treatment. As soon as the *biftecks* were deemed done, Hélène deposited them on the platter on top of the ingredients lying in wait. Swishing is the best way to describe the movement Hélène used to make the meat meet the flavorings and when they were all on the platter, the ensemble was ready to serve. With French fries and a salad . . . What more could you ask for except some nice cool wine?

Granted, the French fries take longer than the *bifteck*. If you don't want to go to the trouble, just have plenty of crusty bread to soak up the sauce and top off the meal with that salad and some cheese.

The preparations I am dealing with use garlic in different ways and the end-products are distinctly different as far as the garlic-taste-factor goes. There are unfortunates who cannot abide by garlic when they see it there, staring them in the nose. They *can* accept it when it is cooked beyond

recognition, so to speak, or smuggled into specialties like chutney or
Worcestershire sauce (which also contains anchovies much to the surprise of
some when it is pointed out to them). If you have to put up with garlic-
phobes, there are two solutions. Cook the hell out of small quantities of it in
large pots of things like spaghetti sauce, or, use it as a part-time flavoring like
this: Cut cloves in half and spear them on toothpicks or place them in a
gadget which is most often used for tea leaves. (Don't use the same gadget
for both if you can help it.) Let the speared slivers stay in just long enough to
impart their zest and remove.

It appears that most breath problems come from actually eating pieces of
garlic rather than ingesting its "essence" by having a piece of it waved
through something and discarded. I must confess that I have never resorted to
the soft-pedaling procedure above. I suggest it in passing only as something
to try if all that's holding a prospective thrill-seeker back is fear of halitosis.
If, in spite of precautions like this, you still have some breath to hide,
chewing parsley will knock out the lion's share. If all else fails, remember the
garlic fan's motto: *"Bad breath is better than none!"*

pollo al ajillo

Pollo al ajillo first slipped through my lips in a gas-station restaurant on the
outskirts of Seville. My Spanish was not all that fluent at the time, but when I
saw and sniffed the platter at an adjoining table and pointed it out to the
waiter, he did the rest. The pieces of chicken bathed in ambrosia lacked only
one refinement: it was quite impossible for me to recognize the morsels. If it
hadn't been for the lack of fingertips in the dish, I would have suspected that
the chef had cut the chicken up blindfolded.

This casual cutting was hardly a major fault, but it's disconcerting to those
who like to pick their particular part of the chicken. The reason behind this

random chopping is that this uniformity of morsel size allows each piece to have its full share of flavor and "doneness." Such anatomy anonymity no longer bothers me in the slightest. Whenever I get back to Spain, I make a bee-line for the nearest bistro to order more of the same. It's easy to try this out at home and here's how:

Massacre a chicken or two according to how many people you want to feed. Cubical pieces about 1½ to 2 inches to a side are a convenient size. Leave the bones in. Coat the bottom of a copious frying pan with a small pool of olive oil and heat it up with a few slivers of garlic for the first kiss of the magic ingredient. Before the slivers get too dark, remove them and toss the chicken into the pan. It won't need any flour or seasoning beyond some salt and pepper. If the pieces are uniform within reason, they will all be cooked at the same time and when they are, take them out and put them somewhere away from the cat (or dog) where they won't cool off too much.

Here comes the fun. While the oil is bubbling away, drop in at least 20 medium-sized cloves of garlic which you have cut into tiny pieces. Spanish chefs usually cut the garlic in little round slices for dishes like this so that there will be something to munch on with the chicken. Minced would be too fine for the right effect. Be very careful now not to overcook. If the oil is hot enough, you can remove the pan from the fire and swish it around until the garlic begins to go 14 carat. At this point, toss the chicken back in, salt and pepper it lightly, if it needs any more, and mix around thoroughly so as to coat the bird with the herb. Return the pan to the stove and as soon as it gets hot, pour a cup of sherry over the whole works. By tilting the pan so that the sherry leaks to the edge, you can get it to flame up, which not only looks spectacular but also terminates in the ultimate taste titillation.

Don't try the flaming bit in cramped quarters, but do leave the pan on the fire just long enough for the sherry to get good and hot, stirring all the while, of course.

Flaming things is much easier on a gas burner than an electric one. With gas, once the alcohol has heated up, it will catch when introduced to the open flame. But, letting it leak onto an electric burner can get messy or fail to work altogether. If you're stuck with electricity, use a match and apply it before the alcohol has boiled out of the wine.

As for the sherry — medium does it for me. Oloroso is too sweet, and Fino, a good Fino, is too expensive and not hearty enough to give the plate a pleasing punch. Have plenty of good bread and/or French fries to soak up the juices and a green salad to cut them. Unless you are a surgeon, you'll have to use your fingers to help you pick the bones clean, and you will want to. Finger-bowls will come in handy. Cool jug wine goes well with this dish. In spite of all the garlic, the overall effect is not as one-sided as you'd imagine. Like Gilroy, garlic capital of the world, *pollo al ajillo* has to be inhaled to be believed.

VOULEZ-VOUS DINER AVEC MOI?

poulet à l'ail

If you haven't skipped to another chapter, you may be just as much of a garlic-head as I am. In this event, I couldn't sleep at night without revealing yet another ravishing garlic chicken dish. This time, it's a French treatment— *poulet à l'ail*—for me, the ultimate garlic triumph. Its taste is altogether different from that of *pollo al ajillo* but is just as beguiling in its own way. The garlic flavor comes at you from a different direction. It is quite possible that one might turn you on and the other off. The same can be said for the two nationalities and their countries. I love them both, the people and their nations, but in different ways. So if one version doesn't get it for you, try the other.

For this recipe, I take advantage of American convenience presentations which enable us to buy pieces of chicken rather than the whole bird. I know that the meat is more expensive this way and that there are those who allow as how *some* pieces might come from defective birds. However, I have been persuaded by Frank Perdue (our East Coast doyen of mass-hatched poultry) that anything he sells has got to be good or else. Experience has proved to my satisfaction that his product is the next best thing to home-grown and a helluva lot easier to deal with. I'm not a leg man, in matters fowl, and wings —though long on taste—are short on meat. Thighs (a.k.a. second-joints) suit me fine. Frank puts them up in 6-packs and that's what I'm giving you details on.

Salt and pepper six thighs and drop them into a casserole in which you've melted a quarter stick of butter with a splash of oil (mild olive or regular cooking oil of your choice). When they are gold top and bottom, put on the lid and let them simmer for about 10 minutes. This will give you time to peel

the cloves from two medium-sized heads of garlic. Mash the garlic but don't mince or slice it. Take the chicken out and shove it in the stay-warm part of your oven or some other suitable place to keep it warm. Throw the mashed garlic into the casserole and cook it over low heat. It is advisable to stir it constantly with a wooden spoon. Not only will the wooden spoon not scratch up your utensil but it will also let you know when the garlic is done enough. When the garlic starts sticking to the spoon, it has cooked sufficiently. This clinging syndrome surprised me when I first heard about it but, having seen it work every time, I have become a believer. Now, pour in half a cup of white wine, stoke up the heat and keep it on the boil for 3 minutes. At this point, put the chicken back in, pour a cup and a half of scalding milk on top, stir briefly, and put the lid back on. Turn down the heat.

Get out some sour cream. Take half a cup of it and add to it a tablespoon of cornstarch, which you can dissolve in just enough water to make it liquid. When the chicken appears done (about a quarter of an hour), mix some of its sauce with the sour cream and cornstarch and pour the combination into the casserole. Turn the heat up again and cook—stirring vigorously for another 3 minutes. There is a tendency for this thickened sauce to separate but vigorous stirring will minimize the chances. If you want to take the chicken out again while you are thickening the brew, it will make your stirring easier and more efficient. No matter how it appears, it will be better than good.

some like it hot!

Now that I've gotten part of my garlic hang-up in print, I'll move on to another area warm to my heart and various other innards—things hot and spicy. If you can't handle garlic or hot pepper, you'll have to bide some time. On the other hand, if you enjoy dishes that moisten your forehead and bring tears to your eyes, hang on.

Before I get into any specific dish, I want to mention in more detail the delightful condiment, developed in old Iberia: *Piri-Piri*, Portugal's spicy answer to the blatant shout of Mexico's Jalapenos. It's a bit more subtle than some of the sauces sprinkled on in New Orleans and Nairobi, but it's pungent, pleasant and pace-changing. I try to keep some on hand at all times. It makes a very fine addition to the grilled skewerfuls mentioned in the Garden Party and the fish dishes in the previous sections. It is very popular with guests who prefer spice in their life.

Piri-Piri is easily concocted. It is an elixir of hot peppers, olive oil, lemon and bay leaf. I guarantee that it will transform a dull dish of just about anything into a real taste teaser. My nephew walked off with the house flagon on his last visit from Philadelphia. My niece pretends she'd rather have it than new Guccis for Christmas. Her chances of the former were far in excess

of the latter and so I set about steeping a ration for her on the spot. This is how I did it.

I took about 15 little red peppers from my kitchen windowsill pepper tree and dropped them into a glass jar. The pepper tree in question is one of the decorative houseplants that show up in our supermarkets, mainly in the fall. They are called "Ornamental Christmas" or "Fiesta Peppers." If you can't get them where you live, some good old hot, dried or fresh peppers from elsewhere will do. I find my pepper tree, all 15 inches of it, not only ornamental but very useful. A slice of lemon went next, then a bay leaf and to complete the potion, a cup of olive oil. With a nice tight lid and an occasional shake, in one month, I had a lively antidote to any jaded palate that came our way.

In case your red peppers are longer than the half-inch ones on my tree, you'll have to cut down on their number. I haven't found any larger ones that pack more punch, but some are just as powerful. Use *piri-piri* sparingly — or lavishly whenever a dish doesn't turn out the way you expected it to. *Piri-piri* is much more interesting than plain old Tabasco sauce and marries well with many Creole dishes too.

Incidentally, hot peppers changed my whole outlook on tuna fish sandwiches. A friend persuaded me to try one of his "specials," which he made with mayonnaise, chopped onions and Jalapeno peppers. It was so good that I didn't even mind his store-bought mayo and supermarket bread.

Now, I make my own version with the bread and mayonnaise I prefer. I don't even have to buy Jalapenos. I use a few of the little red ones fresh from my pepper plant. They must be chopped finely and well distributed throughout the mixture. I use a teaspoon or so of vinegar to mash them in before I add them to the rest. Be sure to wash your hands right after cutting up the peppers. Pepper juice residue can sting like the devil if it gets near your eyes, which you might want to rub after chopping up the onions.

a trip to the khyber pass

Unless you make direct contact with one of the pieces of pickled pepper in your pint of *piri-piri*, you won't run a big risk of uvula burn-out from it. On a world scale of 1 to 10, it rates about a 6.5. When you are ready to move into the hot lane, you'll have to go up the scale through Mexican on your way to the ultimate surprises awaiting you on first dipping into something Pakistani. There are no flies on Indian and Szechwan cooking, as far as heat goes that is, but Far East export efforts are usually watered down considerably once they have crossed the oceans to our shores.

I have no personal experience of the Far East, *in situ*, so my credibility has to depend on what happened to me occidentally one evening at a table in the *Khyber Pass*. That's the name of an Indo-Pakistani establishment in Bute

Street, London. Whether the staff were getting back at Colonials or accommodating ex-patriates is debatable, but one thing is certain, punches are not pulled in the pepper department.

Many of the *Khyber Pass* chicken dishes were available in "mild," "normal" and "hot." I was feeling adventurous but a bit disappointed that my favorite spot, the *Bangkok* restaurant across the street, had been "overbooked" and was not able to accommodate me that evening. Used to somewhat subtle Thai seasoning at the *Bangkok* and expecting similar cuisine at the *Khyber Pass*, I felt no qualms about requesting the "hot" version from my Indian waiter. His eye-blink rate rose to fever pitch. After his Adam's apple went back in place, he asked me if I were sure that I really wanted "hot." He was very hesitant in allowing such a rash choice by an obvious Westerner and suggested "mild." We compromised on "normal," but not without a lot more cautioning that I might find "normal" a bit risky. Fortunately, he had left me a large side dish of fire-extinguishing yoghurt and cucumbers or I might not have made it past the first mouthful. Anyone serving a "normal" hot dish like that one, in the U.S., would be taken to court. I managed to eat most of it. After the initial shock wore off, I found it quite enjoyable. It was a little like eating in a self-induced sauna but it was good. I'm sure I lost more weight than I gained that meal.

While I have not yet encountered anything quite like the *Khyber Pass* in the U.S.A., I have been alerted to an adobe restaurant in Truth or Consequences, New Mexico. According to Mike, a well-traveled Bostonian friend, there are four shades of hot there, the coolest of which is all that should be tackled by anyone but a native. Mike went for the next above mild and said that had it not been for a handy, three-foot loaf of bread, he would have needed a mouth transplant. Unfortunately, he pointed out, to get the bread in to muffle the fire, it was necessary to open his mouth. This is like puffing a bellows in the fireplace. In a case like this, you could take on liquid through a straw with your mouth closed but who wants to sip three gallons of beer that way without stopping, which is about what it would take. Be careful.

Why, then, would anyone in his or her right mind want to play with fire in food? Aside from misguided machos and masochists, there are many of us who enjoy highly spiced hot foods because they taste good and make us feel great. Contrary to rumors, it is still possible to enjoy bland food after learning to like the hot stuff. It's probably possible to o.d. your palate permanently by popping pepper, but it isn't necessary or wise to go to that extent.

Enjoyment aside, there are other benefits to hot pepper. If you are in the tropics, where hot food is close to universal, spicy food will make you feel good and help you bear the heat coming from outside. I didn't have to read research to find this out. First-hand experiences around the Caribbean convinced me long ago. It's folklore down there that pepper is good for you and U.S. doctors have finally come to the same conclusion. Eating lots of *capsicum* (doctor-talk for hot pepper) will help prevent *thromboembolism* (more doctor-talk for blood clots blocking blood vessels). Most gringoes who stick to bland food in Mexico (and other tropical places) will eventually hear from Montezuma. Chances of encountering this sort of discomfort are reduced considerably by indulging in highly seasoned "hot" foods. The peppers and things neutralize the unfriendly bacteria hanging about the less-than-pristine lettuce leaves, they say. So much for all those warnings I received in childhood about too much pepper.

Far be it from me to advocate pouring pepper on everything. Guests who re-season food I've prepared before they even sample, rarely get invited back. Hot recipes, where pepper belongs, have other spices to be noticed too, and a well made dish will taste a lot more than just "hot." And, let's face it. There are many people who simply cannot handle much pepper for physical reasons. No one loses face by under-doing the heavy heat items. One can always have additional condiments on the table to be added *after* tasting. Generally, a spicy dish will be accompanied by something innocuous like rice and be complemented by various side dishes. All of these can allay the volcanic aura. When I prepare a curry, I try to have eight or ten of these extras to sprinkle on at various moments during a meal.

The ultimate in this form of eating is achieved in a *rijsttafel*, something the Dutch have joined with the Indonesians in making known to selected pockets of the world. They took delight in covering every inch of a dining table with loads of little plates of garnishes. I experienced a *rijsttafel* in the Hague and have never been the same since. You don't have to go to Indonesia or even Holland to take advantage of this idea.

author's curry

Curry provides an ideal way to deal with either meat or fish. Though often curries are used to sidetrack leftovers from a trip to the garbage, there is nothing to prevent you from starting off with virgin material. Of the two possibilities, I suggest meat until you get the hang of things. Fish is more delicate and its cooking time(s) more critical. Lamb is standard overseas, but I usually use pork because its taste, to me, is just right for curry. Chicken is second choice because it adapts well to curry and it's cheap. It gives you a good chance to use up the rest of the "Oven-Stuffer." I use available basic vegetables and fruits—onions, celery, raisins, ginger, green and/or red sweet peppers, garlic, coconut, carrots, whatever vegetables are in the hydrator—an apple, sometimes some lemon and, of course, curry.

(For a rundown on the why's and what's-ins of curry, have a glance at section 6: "Seasonings and Spices." Meanwhile, it's time to get on with fixing supper.)

I start up by frying the onions in a bit of oil and then adding the other vegetables. I cut the apple into wedges and toss them in along with slivers of ginger. While everything is softening up, I put in a generous spoonful of curry to make the kitchen smell good. I once had a house guest whose previous curry experience had led him to request a peanut butter sandwich for lunch. After the first aromas of the magic powder began to circulate, he weakened visibly. When he saw the side dishes begin to appear, he caved in completely and asked to be counted in for the curry. He's been asking for a repeat every time he comes back to see us.

At this point, I like to put in some coconut. If I have a fresh one, I use it along with its milk. Otherwise, I use store-bought shredded. If the pieces of meat I am using have not already been cooked, I sear them in a bit of oil in another pan. About the time the coconut has sunk out of sight, I throw in the meat and several more spoonfuls of curry and, occasionally, a lemon half. You'll have to learn from experience how much flavor you can handle.

Though it can be found in paste form, most of our curry comes to us as powder and is available in different degrees of hotness. I suggest beginning with a low-key curry—then you can hot it up later on as you see fit. With the powder sitting on top of everything, I pour on whatever wine is handy and stir things up.

It's a good idea to check occasionally for dryness. When necessary, I add more wine or water and more curry at intervals. I have myself convinced that by adding a little curry from time to time, rather than a whole lot at once, I get a fuller range of flavor in the end result.

Cooking time is quite flexible but an hour will be plenty to get it done. In the last fifteen minutes or so, I put on the rice (see Nicerice) and add some sherry to the curry. It adds just the right amount of sweetness to set off all those pungent items.

If you've got company, now is the time to put them to work. Get out little plates and saucers and have them help you cut, chop or grate any or all of the following except those which can be used as they are: bananas, coconut, chives, lemon, hard-boiled eggs, ginger (crystalized or *finely* minced fresh), almonds, peanuts (cashews if you've got 'em), green peppers, raw onions, burnt onions as described in the "emergency spaghetti sauce," cucumber slices in yoghurt or sour cream with cumin, raisins—both colors and soaked a bit in sweet wine or spirits—and anything else that strikes your fancy. Chutney is also a must.

Two more items are good with curry, but you'll have to buy them in a specialty shop. Bombay duck (which is actually dried fish and not to everyone's taste), and *poppadums*. *Poppadums* are worth having just for the fun of getting them ready, but they are also very good to crunch with curry. They are large wafers about the size of Mexican *tortillas* which you pop into a hot oiled frying pan one at a time. Almost on contact, they pop into large crisp wafers and will amaze anyone who sees them for the first time. Serve everyone a bowl of rice, ladle on the curry and start passing the side dishes. Cold beer is best with this conglomeration.

NOTE: Stir frying is becoming more and more popular these days and a rapid curry may be achieved by its use. However, I find that the longer curry simmers away, the better it becomes. The various flavors meld in such a way that individual tastes don't jump out and take the limelight. A proper curry, for me, is not a short-order dish where a few pieces of meat are drenched with a "curry" sauce and served as such, but rather is a more carefully orchestrated opus that has had time to gain character.

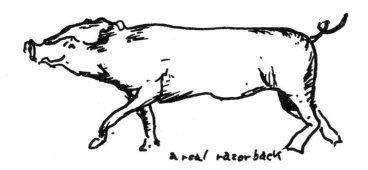

a real razorback

virginia ham

If all the Virginia ham that shows up in one-arm joints around the country actually came from Virginia, that state would have to stretch from the Potomac to the Colorado and be full of pigs to boot. Chances of finding the real thing in posh eateries are even slimmer because real Virginia hams are not only scarce but they often have too much taste for some pampered palates. To give you an idea of how it gets around, a friend reports from Sao Paulo, Brazil, that on the menu of the fancy El Dorado restaurant he visited, there were three words he could understand: "Virginia Ham" and some soft drink whose brand name escapes my memory. He said that the ham wasn't bad, but that the pig who grew it never saw the light of day north of the equator.

The U.S.A. used to have good hams everywhere and still doubtless does, out in the sticks, but try to find them in city markets! In the East, and much of the rest of the world, Virginia has long held the reputation for the best in hams, in particular those labeled "Smithfield." Competition got so fierce, a while back, that ham curers started sleeping in their plants. To leave a smokehouse unguarded was an open invitation for jealous rivals to slip in under the cover of night and torch the operation. Smoked hams were one thing, but incinerated ones were not good for business.

Rivalry got to the point, in 1926, that the state of Virginia stepped in and passed legislation decreeing what could be legally called a Smithfield Ham — a sort of *appellation controlée* like the one used by the French to hold down counterfeit wines. The Virginia state government defined the area where the approved hogs could be raised — namely, the peanut belt which covers parts of Virginia and North Carolina. It insisted that they be fed peanuts and, when the time came, that they take their ultimate dirt-nap on Virginia soil, in Smithfield no less.

As of now, there are only four processors authorized to use the term "Genuine Smithfield" on their Virginia hams. They are V. W. Joyner, Smithfield Ham & Products Co., Smithfield Packing Co., and Gwaltney. They are all located in Smithfield and I'll tell you shortly how to get in touch with them and other packers who have good hams too.

Unfortunately, our modern, time-saving, ordinary ham-processing methods have succeeded in giving us mostly an insipid, pink product that bears as much relation to good old country ham as spongy American bread does to the real thing. That also goes for the Polish and Danish and all those other tinned things that are imported as ham. Southern Europe still indulges in a proper cure, one which often takes two years or more. Observant travelers can see hams on the roofs in sunny areas of back country Spain. *Prosciutto* from Italy can be found here, but the best of all — *serrano* from Spain and *presunto de Chaves* from Northern Portugal — are not imported in "legal" quantities. Neither is *jambon cru*, country ham turned out in various pockets of the French countryside and considered, by Smithfield experts, as the best they've tasted anywhere, away from home of course.

The reason we don't get to see these marvels is supposedly because they are cured but *not* cooked. We just don't allow uncooked meat into the U.S. How Italian grocers get all that *prosciutto* past the customs' hawkeyes is a mystery, but at the price it goes for, it could be arriving via private jets.

We still have good ham in this country and if you want to take the trouble to get it, you can. Mind, I am very subjective about this matter — one important requirement is that it has to have a lot more taste than the waxed paper it's sold in at the local deli. We get our hams by mail. The Virginia-oriented portion of our family acknowledges the existence of other well-cured products from places like Kentucky and Tennessee, but we still hold out for something from down home when we want the best. Maybe you'll care to join us in our pursuit of flavor from the good old days. Remember that Virginia has been exporting hams to Europe since the 1600s, so they must be doing something right.

finding the right cure

They've been curing hams pretty much the same way, down South, since the early settlers learned how to do it from the Indians. In a land where tradition dies hard, there are still some firms that give more than lip-service to the time-tested method. Personal experience still leads me to believe that current cure time is much less than it used to be. Another thing that dies hard is memory, and we firmly believe, in our family, that present-day hams are not as good as they used to be.

Nostalgia can be tricky. Sometimes I wonder whether things ever were as good as they "used to be." I'm quite sure, however, that genuine current-day Virginia hams are much better than the many bogus ones foisted off on the public as the real thing.

A Virginia ham is dry cured and may or may not be smoked for more flavor. The dry cure consists primarily of rubbing the ham with salt and letting it hang around for at least six months. The rubbing salt may be spiked with pepper and brown sugar and maybe a bit of molasses, depending on the curer's own particular method.

When a Virginia ham gets to you, the first thing you will have to do is soak it. It then gets boiled and later baked. At the boiling stage, I put in a bay leaf or two, a few tablespoons of black molasses and half a cup of vinegar. The brew left when the ham is removed goes to the freezer in readiness for cooking string beans or some more of that black bean soup I was telling you about in Section 2.

When baking time comes (actually, it's only glazing because the ham has been thoroughly cooked by boiling), it's quick and easy. The ham gets peeled and the remaining exterior fat gets rubbed with a mixture of brown sugar, bread crumbs, dry mustard and ground cloves. If you prefer to use whole cloves, go right ahead—they look pretty—but the ground ones are more practical in distributing the flavor and less risky for your molars. Don't remove much of the fat with the skin—for some of us, it's as important as the lean. While it's in the oven (400 degrees for 15 minutes or until it looks right) be sure to baste a few times with accumulating melted sugar and fat. This will help keep the bread crumbs from burning black—something which has happened to me more than once, I regret to confess.

Before serving the ham, make sure that it's cool enough so that you can slice it thinly and not have that remaining delicious fat fall off. Heavy-handed guests, who trim portions thicker than razor blades, should be invited to leave the carving board at once. They can have all they want to eat, but proper house rules exact Gillette proportions. I make my sandwiches without anything other than ham and a little *lightly* buttered bread, but there are those who must have mustard.

Generally, a Virginia ham will last several weeks in a cool spot. If you don't have a chilly pantry, you may resort to the refrigerator. In the fullness of time, some of the exterior, especially the tail end, gets too hard to enjoy in the usual way. You can chew it as you would "jerky," but there's another way to put it to good use. Grind the hard pieces with mayonnaise and pickles and use it as a sandwich spread. It puts ordinary deviled ham to shame. If the ham is real dry, dribble in some juice from the pickle jar too as you grind it.

mustard butter

Here's the way we used to cut the mustard in the family shop I have told you about. We mixed mayonnaise with softened butter (one mayo to two butter) and when smooth, added wet mustard. The mustard has to go in last or funny things happen to the mixture. As for the mayonnaise, use homemade unless you care to settle for second best.

Mustard butter can be made up in quantity and kept in the refrigerator for all kinds of sandwiches. We tried to sell the idea to Mister Gulden Senior, back in the '50's, but not being as sharp as his mustard, he didn't take us on. The secret has remained dormant all this time and somebody out there could make a killing with this concoction in our gourmet age. Please send royalties directly to author.

ham by mail

The 1986 genuine uncooked Virginia ham price hovered over the two- to three-dollar-a-pound neighborhood, including postage and the huge ham bone inside. The longer the cure, in general, the tastier the ham and the higher the price. Ham loses weight in curing and cooking. It takes time and care to prepare, but it's worth the money and effort. By the time you are finished, it will still cost you less per pound than a deluxe cut of raw steak. It is *supposed* to be served in thin slices. If you can read the New York Times classifieds through it, you're doing fine. A little will go a long way, *after* you've pigged out on your initial fix, during which you might get carried away by the novelty of something so full of flavor.

You can obtain a list of some of the outfits that will ship Virginia hams to you on request by writing to:

The Virginia Pork Industry Commission
801 Washington Building
1100 Bank Street,
Richmond, VA 23219

Enclose a No. 10, self-addressed, stamped envelope and you'll soon be rewarded with a gold mine of very usual information including folklore and all the details necessary for making your ham table-ready. There are recipes and instructions on how to carve.

The hams you locate by using this list are less expensive than any I have seen advertised in the flashy catalogs from gourmet houses. You can rest assured that they will be "the real thing," too.

We've tried several houses and the best hams we have had recently came from Gwaltney. Phone 804-357-3131 or write to

Gwaltney of Smithfield Ltd.
P.O. Box 489
Smithfield, VA 23430

They have two categories — the more expensive one, "Genuine Smithfield" (about $40), comes as close to archetypical as we have encountered of late. At $10 less, their "Williamsburg" model is closer to the regular country ham found in other markets. These are uncooked.

For comparison's sake, we recently splurged on a Genuine Smithfield *cooked* at $50. It was superb. It was done to a "Tee" and boned (a tremendous advantage for easier carving and cutting down waste). In fact, the only disadvantages I found were that they had removed more of my beloved fat than I would have. That's probably a lot better for me, but I do like the fat almost as much as the lean. The lack of the ham juice left from boiling is another consideration if you want some for a soup base. Well, you win some and you lose some, but you'll still be eatin' high on the hog when you have a Smithfield ham on your table.

If I have trod on some sensitive toes out there from other ham havens, let me know what you have discovered. Hey, you can send me one if you want to do a little proselytizing. I am always ready to try something different. It's just that I like Virginia ham so much, I haven't really bothered to go farther afield to improve on it. I still wish that they would cure them longer, the way they did before but . . . nobody's perfect these days.

marinating

The word marinate comes from versions of *mariner, marinare* and *marinar,* old French, Italian and Spanish words which sailors used in describing how food was preserved to survive at sea. At its most simple, and least appetizing, it meant putting meat in brine, where it stayed until used. Since then, there have been many modifications designed to turn taste and toughness more tempting. Though still more prevalent in Europe than in the U.S., marinating is growing increasingly popular on this side of the Atlantic. You can even find a selection of marinades in supermarkets these days, although why anyone would not prefer to make them at home defeats me. They are a cinch to concoct and cost a lot less when homemade. Since refrigeration has pretty much eliminated marination for preservation, what has revived interest in it for us lies more in taste transformation and tenderization.

The ingredients used depend on the kind of food to be marinated and the taste of the cook. Some form of vinegar or wine (or both) is essential for the chemical action of tenderizing. Oil adds taste and keeps spicy flavors from escaping and unfriendly elements from getting in. While the process is taking place, the oil floats to the top and keeps adventurous flies from sinking into the marinade if you have forgotten to cover it over. As for the taste, anything goes. Thyme, rosemary, salt and pepper, bay leaves, basil, parsley, onions, garlic, carrots, cloves and even juniper berries can all take part in the show.

In standard meat marinating, the pieces of meat are given the once over with a bit of salt and pepper and placed on a bed of chopped carrots and onions. Some prefer not to use salt—either for dietary reasons or the unsealing effect of salt on the meat, which can cause its natural juice (and flavor) to seep out and get lost in the marinade. If you feel the need, add the salt later when you cook the meat. Pour oil over the ensemble next—it will help the next ingredients to adhere. Add the bay leaf crumbled or whole, the garlic whole, sliced or minced. Spread other herbs and spices of your choice around the meat. Then, being careful not to float the spices off into one lump, pour on vinegar and/or wine (even a dash of Cognac for special dishes). I frequently add some lemon juice, too. Proportions of wine to oil go from 3 to 1 and on up. Some marinades don't contain oil at all.

You don't have to submerge the meat in juice, but you should turn it every now and then so that the mixture gets a chance to work all over. Use a dish deep enough so that the meat won't peek over the top, but try not to leave much space around the edge of whatever you are marinating. Cover it over with a lid or plastic wrap or both.

The minimum time for the marinade to work depends on the temperature. Two and a half hours at room temperature will give a noticeable effect. Longer than four days can wreck things. I like to leave marinades in the refrigerator overnight, mainly because of the cats and dogs. Even though they don't care for vinegar and garlic, they are so curious that they sometimes investigate a little too closely and make things go bump in the night.

Don't spare the plastic wrap if you are using the refrigerator. Use more than one thickness so that the marinade's strong aroma won't spread through your other stored victuals and into the freezer to flavor your ice.

When you get ready to cook the meat, you must remove it from the bath and dry it off. The temptation to cook the whole combination is to be avoided. We don't want to waste the ingredients from the marinade, but they have to stand by for later use. If the marinee is cooked in the marinade, you can wind up with a sour stew instead of what you might want to turn into a ravishing roast.

NOTE: Under *iscas de porco* I have for you a recipe using a marinade which has caused many who can't stand liver to take a new pledge, in its favor. In this method, the marinade will be used for a sauce but *not* to cook the meat. But first, a few words on liver, a meat that very few people seem to be neutral about.

liver can be great

Whenever we have guests from France, I eventually steer them to the supermarket. It's lots of fun to see their eyes pop when they drift by the meat counter and check the prices. They really go haywire when they find fresh calves' liver at less than $2 a pound. (It's generally around five times that in France.) Beef liver is even less expensive, and one good reason for this is that many Americans can't stand liver. If the only way they ever had it was anything like what passed for liver in my boarding-school days, I can sympathize with the revulsion. Done to the consistency of combat-boots, it found few eager takers.

The first liver I had in France was a revelation. It was *foie de veau grillé*, grilled calves' liver. Lightly done a couple minutes on each side, it was tender, pink, tasty, topped with lemon juice and parsley and dripping with butter instead of bacon fat. It instantly became clear to me why they could charge so much for it. It was still liver, but what a difference!

Anyone with enough butter and good fresh calves' liver can do it French-style and perhaps convert abounding members of the anti-liver lobby. On the other hand, if you will take a page from the Portuguese, here's another quite different and very delicious way to do a job on liver that will have anyone past puberty coming back for more. Not too many small fry can handle this preparation but don't let that stop you from trying it.

iscas de porco

Iscas (pronounced eesh-kas) are what you would ask for in Portugal. They are thin slices of liver, usually pig's, marinated and cooked. If you are in Brazil, you might choose another word, because in that country, *isca* is the equivalent of "sic 'em" for attack-dogs. For that matter, it means "fish-bait" in Portugal, so you would be wise to specify *iscas de figado* or *iscas de porco*, just in case you wind up on a gastronomic tour of Portuguese fishing villages—a great trip, by the way. *Figado* is the regular word for liver in Brazil and Portugal and *porco* is, of course, pig.

This preparation is also splendid with calves' liver but, if you do it properly, you can save by buying a cheaper kind. In Portugal, they usually make *iscas* with pork liver, which U.S. meat-markets almost have to pay customers to take away in all but ethnic neighborhoods. Here's an Americanized version of *iscas de figado*. Try it; you may like it.

For two or three pounds of liver, make a marinade of red wine, vinegar, garlic, salt and pepper, a bay leaf and olive oil. I often toss in a pinch or sprig of thyme too. Lay the slices in the marinade, cover and let the dish stand 3 hours or *more* at room temperature. Turn the slices over once in a while so they can get full benefit of the marinade. If you plan to leave it much longer than 3 hours, it's better to put it in the refrigerator.

Slowly cook about a quarter pound of bacon in 2 or 3 tablespoons of olive oil! Yes, olive oil! When the bacon is crisp, take it out and let the oil heat up. Remove the *iscas* from their marinade and pat them dry with paper towels. Drop them into the bubbling frying pan and give them two minutes a side — no more — just until they are lightly browned. Take them out, keep them warm and pour the marinade in the pan. Heat it quickly until it is reduced by half. Pour the sizzling sauce over the *iscas* and crumble the bacon on top. Toss on some parsley and serve with fried (or boiled) potatoes and a *hefty* red wine. This is a good chance to use up that leftover "Hearty Burgundy" that's too thick to go with more delicate rations. Follow with a green salad.

NOTE: In Portugal, this would probably be prepared with salt pork instead of bacon — they do have baço but, no matter how they spell it, bacon almost everywhere in Europe is not quite what we expect. Aside from a difference in curing, their bacon is from the loin and ours is from the underbelly. I have found that American bacon is more to our taste in this recipe than salt pork. In Portugal, *iscas* would be one dish of a 3 or 4 course meal but for me, it's enough to get stuffed.

chicken livers

As long as we're into livers, let's go one step further and consider those of the chicken. They represent one of the best meat buys in the market. However, they're no bargain if you don't like 'em. One drawback is texture. They tend to have a mealy feel which sticks to the top of the mouth. I like their flavor, properly subdued. Lightly sautéed in butter with minced garlic and a bit of rosemary, they are dandy. By the time they are warmed through, they are ready for a splash of sherry and a generous portion of sour cream stirred in just long enough to get hot but not cooking. Served on toast, they make a good economical lunch.

As good as they taste done this way, they still have that cling-to-the-roof-of-the-mouth tendency that not everyone can put up with. I have finally found a method that makes them slide down more easily, which might be more to the liking to some. I "borrowed" an idea for chicken livers with pasta from Jeff Smith, the "Frugal Gourmet." I figured he wouldn't mind, since he says he "adopts" others' ideas himself every time he finds something he likes. The jury is still out on which way is best in our house, but here's the other version in case you wish to join us in our deliberations.

You'll need some chicken stock or broth. If you don't have any, a couple of bouillon cubes will make an adequate substitute. Since the liver doesn't take long to prepare, put on a pot of water to boil for some noodles. Then, prepare a roux. Blend equal parts of butter and flour (about a tablespoon of each). Warm up the mixture until it's smooth and the flour has had a chance to cook. (There is a special kind of flour called "Wondra" which will facilitate making a successful roux—more about it in Section 6.) Add the roux to a cup or so of chicken stock or broth. While the roux is thickening the broth, introduce the livers to a frying pan with hot butter and olive oil.

The water should be perking by now, so shovel in the noodles and check the time they require from their package. Squeeze a clove or two of garlic over the livers and sprinkle in herbs of your choice. Sometimes I use just dill —other times I put in rosemary and thyme. Salt and pepper lightly. Keep your eye on the roux, stirring to keep it from burning while you are sautéing the livers. When they have firmed up, add sherry, and slosh around the pan until it bubbles. Take the frying pan off the stove and pour all the juices you can into the sauce, stirring to incorporate them well. The noodles should be done by now. Drain them, divide them up on plates or in bowls, place the livers on the noodles and pour on the sauce. Serve and enjoy.

While it would seem that you might need a couple extra hands to make everything come out at the same time, it's really not as tough as it sounds. The main pitfalls to be avoided are overcooking the livers and over-thickening the sauce. If it doesn't come out right the first time, give the dog a treat and try again.

5 | vegetables and such

Some cooks will knock themselves loop-legged perfecting a fancy sauce or mollycoddling a twenty dollar roast and relegate vegetables to minority status. Have you ever sat down to a beautifully set table, beautiful wines on the sideboard, beautiful silver and china, with beautiful people—and been served a beautiful first course and a beautiful roast whose side dish was unseasoned, boiled string beans or plain boiled spinach. I have. It happens, alas. What a way to kill a meal. There are so many ways to complement good greenery that it is a constant source of amazement to me that more imagination doesn't penetrate to the average kitchen.

A good share of today's vegetables reaches us via the quick-frozen route. As a rule, frozen are superior to fresh, unless you are in an area where fresh means what it says. Frozen or fresh, vegetables need help to show them off at their best. Probably the most vital ingredient to well prepared vegetables is butter. With good butter and a hint of salt and pepper, most cooked vegetables appear at their best. If they haven't come straight from your own garden, you might want to go a bit further in preparation.

Take peas, for example. Everybody eats peas but not everybody makes the effort to improve on just boiling them. Here's a variation that is no trouble at all and the results will have your guests wondering how you did it. Even canned peas do well with it, especially the very small ones. It's so simple that I might not have thought of telling you about it had it not been for my

old friend Marie, who reminds me about them when we get to talking food—
something we do whenever we get together.

Marie was a partner in a little art gallery we opened here in our town.
She's 100% American and another 100% Italian and has raised a family to
match. They *love* to eat and eat what they love—*real* people in the strictest
sense. Peas were on the menu of the first meal they ate at my house—back
when the kids were turning teen-aged. They liked the taste of these peas so
much that when Turkey Day rolls around in November, they won't believe
that it's Thanksgiving unless their Mom puts some on their already sway-
backed table. This is the way Marie and I suggest that you prepare them:

Drain your canned peas or get your frozen ones out of the freezer. Use the
smallest ones you can find, for they are far and away the best. In a saucepan,
melt some butter and toss in a few very thin slices of onion. As the onion
turns golden, add a couple of teaspoons of dry breadcrumbs and keep them
heating until they absorb some butter and start crisping up. Add the peas and
heat until hot. Frozen peas have enough of their own moisture to need
nothing else. If you're lucky enough to have fresh ones, you may have to add
a bit of water.

As simple as this method is, hardly anyone seems to know about it, much
less practice it. I'd bet 50 cents to an old underwear button that you'll be
pleasantly surprised when you try it, too.

Frozen vegetables, by nature, don't require any more water when they're
cooked in a saucepan. All they need is some lubricant to keep from sticking
to the pan. Butter is the ideal cushion—it avoids the burning and imparts the
very best of taste. The onions give the added twist that makes them move
from mundane to magnificent.

If you prefer steaming—probably the best way to get the most out of
vegetables—go right ahead. Just don't present them as is, without seasoning,
unless you're entertaining stick-in-the-mud visitors you don't want to see ever
again.

A lot of people don't like cauliflower. A lot of people have good reason
not to. It is often boiled (whole!) to mush and possibly covered with cheese

TRIVET for STEAMING.

glop which could pass for library paste. To make cauliflower much more appealing and simpler to prepare, try it this way.

First, cut the head into pieces. The resulting florets may not look as spectacular as the entire vegetable, but the cauliflower will undergo far less risk of being overcooked. Steam the pieces until you can almost get a fork into one. This way, cauliflower is an absolute marvel when served hot from the steamer with a lump of melting butter in the middle of each heap of florets. Squeeze on some lemon juice at the table.

Try the same method with broccoli. Peel the stems and put them at the bottom of the steaming trivet because the flowers will be done sooner and you'll be able to take them out first. My personal preference for broccoli is to serve it with oil and vinegar drizzled on top. I like oil and vinegar on asparagus too. After all, butter is better on so many other things. We all have our little personal quirks. Non-violent as I am, I would really like to wring the neck of the character who dreamed up spoiling perfectly good cauliflower with cheese.

Not counting the squash family, about the only other readily available ordinary green vegetable around here is string beans. I like them sort of Italian style—i.e., lightly cooked and served with oregano, sliced onions with oil and vinegar. Cold or hot, I enjoy them that way. The other two-thirds of our family like them with peeled potatoes, cooked to death in ham juice (Virginia ham juice, to be sure) and served with sliced tomatoes and mayonnaise. I must say that they are not at all bad that way, especially when the string beans are as tired as they usually are by the time they reach our markets.

These are simple ideas to put into use, but I haven't noticed many people using them. They will add zest to your meals if you give them a chance.

keeping green vegetables green

There is a simple trick that will work wonders keeping some vegetables green. For example, by plunging broccoli branches in boiling water, you can make them a dynamic green in a matter of seconds. Those of you who have put up vegetables for canning will recognize this as blanching, a necessity for proper preservation. I wondered why it works and this is what I found out:

The sudden concentration of heat drives off the air lurking in and around the leaves and flowers of a vegetable, effectively concentrating our view of the plant pigments. The bright color was there all along but just not highly visible through its atmosphere. The easiest analogy I can dream up is the change in color of a bright blue sky as you move your gaze from overhead towards the horizon. The blue is really the same but it has to be seen through more atmosphere the lower you look and so becomes less blue as your ken leaves the zenith.

After blanching brings on the bright color, more heat will cause chemical reactions which will continue to change the color one way or another. The less time you have to use to cook a vegetable, the less it will change in appearance. So, if you steam, which is the fast way, most vegetables will retain more of their fresh initial hue.

Unfortunately, this won't work with artichokes, the main reason being that they require more time in the heat to get done. I tried plunging one into boiling water as a control and put it into steam with others, unplunged. They all came out the same, rather dull-looking at that. Subsequent experimentation brought out the interesting fact that they do hold their color much better when done in stainless steel, which I recommend for reasons of taste as well as color. Aluminum is particularly bad with artichokes.

Broccoli requires less cooking than artichokes and therefore has a better chance of staying bright. So do other quick-cooking greens, and since crisp vegetables have become the mode these days, a lot of food of late has become more attractive to look at.

Vegetables not only look better when cooked rapidly, they remain more nutritious if too much food value isn't dissipated into water and air. Arguments are legion for both boiling and steaming, with and without covers. A further influence on the end result is the quality of the water used to cook. Soft (alkaline) water breaks down vegetables more quickly than that which is more acid. In a covered pan, the plant acids which are driven off from the vegetables will condense on the lid and fall back into the water, thus delaying the dissolution of pigment (and other qualities) into the cooking liquid. The vitamins saved won't do you any good unless you use the leftover water in soup or something, but the color will be less affected. Using soda to keep things green is a *no-no*. It makes the water too alkaline and leaches out the good parts in spite of its chemical reaction which conserves the green, leading us to think the result is more healthful.

Logically, steaming has several advantages over boiling. Since its temperature is higher than boiling, less will be lost in the decreased time of cooking. When a covered cooking vessel is used, the steam not only works faster but gives back at least some of the goodies to the steamee. By extension, the speed of stir-frying is also likely to get you the most out of whatever you are cooking.

On the other hand, if you prefer to boil, your best bet is to use lots of water and have it really roiling before you drop in the vegetables. This is because the most esthetic damage (change of color) is done in the neighborhood of 160 degrees. A large ratio of boiling water to what's being boiled will dissuade the temperature from dropping to this level, but the extra water will filter off more of the vitamins. Vitamins B and C are the ones most soluble in water. Cutting vegetables in small pieces so that they cook faster doesn't outweigh the further loss of vitamins which then have more surfaces to escape from, but it helps them stay crisp and appetizing. When it's not convenient to stir-fry, I steam for all these reasons. If you are really worried about losing essentials, there are always vitamin pills. My feeling is that if one has to worry about every bite being right, too much of the fun goes out of food—our psyches need nourishment too.

the artichoke

Much has been said about the bravery of the first person to eat an oyster, but rarely do we read about the courage required to get the better of an artichoke and/or who was desperate enough to dare using them for food. Ancient Greeks enjoyed them, but neither the artichoke nor many Greeks came to western America until the early 1900s. Half Moon Bay, just north of Santa Cruz in California, is where they were first transplanted by Italian settlers. Along Route One on the way to San Francisco, there are endless fields of them—the rolling Pacific on one side and artichoke heaven on the other. This hearty comestible member of the daisy family is getting more and more popular with us in spite of its self-defense resources.

The adult artichoke has essentially two ways to get back at a would-be consumer—tiny, little, very sharp thorns at its leaf tips and the choke itself, the fuzzy interior which is to be avoided when eating. It's in April and May that the California farmers ship out their most ferocious and best tasting. On one occasion, I not only stuck myself, while examining some 3-for-89-cent whoppers, but also witnessed them dry-gulch the cashier *and* the bag-boy at the super check-out. Neither one knew what they were. I explained that, once captured and cooked, artichokes are worth every risk, at least to me.

Artichokes are really thistles and they grow all over Europe. When allowed to flower, they produce one of nature's more beautiful creations, rivaling roses and orchids in their splendor. Before blooming, they can reach near basketball proportions in Brittany, which is where the French produce some of the best I've tasted so far. Twice a week, a truckful of them came to Chanzeaux, where I used to live in France. The farmer-driver took great pride in demonstrating to me that his *artichauts* were tender enough to be eaten raw. I could never convince him that I didn't care for them raw, but we ran through the litany of tenderness every time he came, until I finally agreed with him so that we could get on with discussing other global matters like wine and weather.

For some, just the required exfoliation makes artichokes too much trouble to eat. They have to be stripped of their petals, one at a time, and then dipped in sauce and dragged through clenched teeth to extract small scrapings of goodness. The standard French sauce, the one which I stick with, is oil and vinegar with a little salt. The spoon-shaped petals hold just enough liquid to set off their taste. Logical minds would call for dipping with the curved side pointing down, but not everyone agrees on this.

My hosts in Chanzeaux, an American professor and his wife, had a perpetual debate over this procedure—he opted for the curve up (like an upside-down spoon). This, of course, allowed a minimum of vinaigrette to complement the leaves and a maximum to drip on the table and his shirt. Like many couples, they had their squabbles—he used to sing his artichoke-loving kids to sleep at night. She preferred his company by the fire after dinner. One evening she issued a ukase that more than one song and she was leaving home. He acquiesced and sang "99 bottles of beer on the wall," (*all* the way through).

I am a curve up, dip in oil and vinegar, person. That's as much as I like to tamper with artichokes. Hollowing them out and filling them with creamed chicken or bread crumbs and cheese does not get it for me. I have sampled artichoke soup in the California village of Pescadero, where artichokes abound. It was good but . . . give me the simple artichoke for a steady diet.

Cooking artichokes is simplicity itself. They can be boiled or steamed and eaten hot or cold, even luke-warm. About the only advance preparation required, besides rinsing them off, is a little manicuring. Cut off the dried

STEAMER

ends of the stalks so that water or steam can penetrate. Pluck off a *few* of the bottom leaves until you get to the ones with more meat on them. Then slice off the tops. This isn't essential in small artichokes but helps get rid of those pesky thorns in more mature specimens. I like to steam mine so I put them, stems down, on a trivet in a big pot with an inch of slightly salted water in the bottom. The salt is not for flavor but makes the water boil at a higher temperature and thus do its work faster. I cover them with a lid that lets a little steam escape and check often for tenderness.

Mealy artichokes are to be avoided and that's what they can become when they cook too long. If your "other" cook book says 40 minutes, examine them at 20 by sliding a paring knife into the stalks. When it meets little resistance, chances are they are done. Remove from the pan and let them drain *upside-down* so the water collected inside them will drain out. Drag out the oil and vinegar and dip when ready. When you have finished with the petal ends, pare off the fuzzy stuff from the top of the bottom, a.k.a. the heart. This fuzzy stuff is aptly named the "choke" and people have been known to strangle on it. Cut up the heart and drop it into the vinaigrette. For some, this is the best part. Gnawed leaves occupy a lot of table space but artichoke detritus will keep your compost pile happy.

NOTE: A word of caution: If you have a disposal in your kitchen, NEVER use it to get rid of any part of the artichoke unless you are devoted to helping your plumber pay off his mortgage. Artichokes and celery are just two of the fibrous foods that are death on disposals.

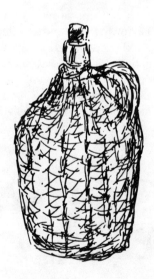

the great artichoke bonus

There is one more piece of artichoke lore which should not go unheralded. Artichokes will make jug red into something eminently potable and can transform a minor wine into a real treat. There is a substance, *cynarin*, in the plant which alters the taste buds, temporarily, and can improve the taste of various foods, and drinks—particularly wine.

The change of taste is not the same for everyone. For most people, it makes things taste sweeter and this is not always desirable. The after-effects can linger long enough to last through a meal. If you are planning other dishes that might suffer from this alteration, have the artichokes last. I usually have them as a first course because I'm usually juggin' it for the whole meal. I enjoy the new twists any lingering taste modifier can chance to produce. By the same token, if a menu is to be highlighted by a really great vintage, it would be wise for all of us to skip artichokes altogether for that fiesta.

Note: The Italians make *Cynar*, an aperitif using artichokes as a base. I have not found that it enhances anything. Sipping *Cynar* before dining is like starting a meal with Moxie.

jerusalem artichokes

In case you live in a part of the country where artichokes refer mainly to Jerusalem artichokes, be advised that they are completely different articles. The Jerusalem model is actually the root of a North American sunflower. The Jerusalem handle is thought to be a deformation of the *girasole*, which is Italian for sunflower and means literally turn with the sun. This is a habit with sunflowers and you can observe it for yourself if you have the time to spare to watch a field of them rotate during the day. It's worth it, at least once, if you're passing through Kansas or Córdoba (the one in Spain), where they grow a lot of them for their seeds, not their roots.

In France, a very close cousin of the Jerusalem artichoke is the *topinambour*, a name borrowed along with the plant from a tribe in Brazil. In Chanzeaux, among other places, there is a root which can be distinguished (visually) from Jerusalem artichokes only by its size. My upside-down-petal-pusher host was convinced that the cartfuls of these roots, actually destined to feed livestock, had to be the same vegetable he grew up with back home in Indiana. The fertile French soil just made them grow bigger, he reasoned. Nothing would do until he convinced the rest of us to try them. We did. We had to leave all the windows open for two days after that experience. They had a slightly similar flavor but the cooking emitted an industrial strength aroma not unlike the atmosphere around Newark on the New Jersey Turnpike.

the seasonal glut

Fortuitously, galley time for this opus has coincided with the moment of peak production for our home garden. In other words, I'm up to my eyebrows in tomatoes and experimenting with ways to eat them at breakfast, lunch and dinner without turning into one myself. It's too bad that they are edible for such a short season, but it's better to make the most of them while they're available. That goes for zucchini, too. If anything, they are even easier to grow than tomatoes, but a little zucchini goes much farther than a lot of tomatoes, for us, and we try to keep the brakes on our resident gardener, José, when he gets that zucchini-planting look in his eyes. There are just so many people you can thrill by giving them your surplus zucchini before they start paying you back with theirs.

To take full advantage of all those fresh, ripe tomatoes, requires a little more imagination than that needed to come up with salads and sandwiches. Here are a few suggestions, should you have the good fortune to find yourself laden with the fruits of an overflowing garden.

We may no longer think of tomatoes as fruit because commerce has deemed otherwise. In the 1800s, as now, tomatoes were sometimes imported. Initially, as fruits, they were not subject to import duty. U.S. growers resorted to "protectionism" by taking the matter to court, the U.S. Supreme Court at that. To make our country a little greener, tomatoes were thenceforth classified as taxable veggies and so it goes.

Starting in at breakfast, I take a leaf from the English who, despite their less than savory reputation for cooking, are acknowledged masters of the day's first meal. They get good little tomatoes most of the year from the Channel Islands and you will quite often find them served at breakfast, keeping company with eggs, bacon or ham, and a mushroom or two. The tomatoes are simply cut in half and fried right along with the rest, eggs going in last, of course, because they require very little time to cook.

Recently, I have been frying whole pans of tomatoes for breakfast, without eggs. I get the bacon going. I cut the ends off the tomatoes and slice them in half-inch rounds and put them in with the bacon. I add a little pepper, some oregano and, towards the end, a splash of Marsala. With toast, they start the day off right. I must say, however, that a glass of wine goes better with them than a cup of coffee. Since I usually start my day at five a.m. with a pot of black coffee, by seven o'clock I'm ready for something more substantial. Having already had my caffeine rushes for the day, I indulge in a glass from the grape.

At lunch, a little garden fry is nice. Onions first, in butter and/or oil, then small slices or chunks of zucchini and slivers of red bell peppers. I mince garlic over the lot and add herbs, usually rosemary and thyme. Green peppers are good in this too. If you have the time and patience to broil and peel them first, they are even tastier. Charred and peeled peppers are one of the ingredients that make an antipasto so appealing to many diners.

With very little alteration, the garden fry can be converted to a *ratatouille*. This is a French term for a gross stew and is pronounced "rra-tah-toooo-ya." In the south of France, it has become a meatless stew of tomatoes, *courgettes* (a near relative of zucchini), peppers, eggplant, garlic and onions. A certain mystique has developed about preparing *ratatouille*. Even though all the ingredients are eventually mingled, classic recipes call for individual handling of each along the way. I don't think this complication is really necessary.

I lived many years in *ratatouille* country and enjoyed it no matter how it was prepared. I have found, however, that the extra work often prescribed in complicated versions just isn't worth it unless you're in a *ratatouille* cook-off, seeking a big prize. As a result, I am offering a recipe, translated from the French housewives' cooking bible called *Je Sais Cuisiner* (I Know How to Cook). The French ingredients were given in the metric system, which accounts for the funny weights involved. It has the standard ingredients of all *ratatouille* recipes with none of the hassle. Everything is dumped in a pot, unceremoniously, and put on the back burner for a couple of hours.

The bare-bones recipe in the back of this book was probably written by someone from the north of France and was destined for people who already know their way around the kitchen. I say the north of France because the *Provençale* modifier suggests the area around Nice, where this dish was invented. It just so happens that the *Niçoises* don't peel the eggplant! It's hard to believe that the author didn't call for the onions to be sautéed slightly first nor did she mention any *herbes*. The last two suggestions I highly recommend.

The real secret about a *ratatouille* is that it tastes much, much better the second day, cold or hot. I prefer cold but not everyone does. Anyway, this is a good starting point for you to perfect your own version and its simplicity makes it more tempting to try than the complicated instructions I've seen in most American French cookbooks.

Not wishing to foist off an un-tested formula on you, I made the *ratatouille* just as explained in the *Je Sais Cuisiner* handbook. Well, almost. I thought I had some zucchini on hand but when it came down to the nitty-gritty, there wasn't a zucchini in sight. I figured, why not try it without and see what the results were. We had some hot from the pot and then cold the next day. A decided success it was!

Incidentally, I had planned to fry up some zucchini and add it to see what difference it made. I went to the A & P, bought a few, put them on the scale by the check-out, *paid for them*, and left for home. Alas, they stayed on the scale. Obviously, fate had ordained that I pass on a new recipe, the one in the recipe section *sans* zucchini. I would add that I feel the addition of water is superfluous, there being plenty in the various ingredients already. I do feel that cooking the onions down a bit in the olive oil is a must, however, and this will also prevent scorching of the next things to join the crowd.

In between paragraphs, I am in the process of putting up a batch for use next winter when fresh tomatoes are history. I am restraining myself from throwing in batches of herbs — without them, it has still proved to be very tasty, but my next batch will have some. I think that the eggplant peel is doing the trick of imparting sufficient flavor. You can have a lot of fun having guests try to guess what you added to make the dish so good, when what you've really done is leave out the zucchini.

tomatoes *à la provençale*

Ratatouille is the essence of *Provence* and so are tomatoes à la Provençale, another favorite of mine. They are a cinch to prepare. The following method will render even winter supermarket tomatoes edible though it's preferable to have a go at them when you can get the real things.

Pour a hooker of olive oil on a baking tray (with edges, this can get juicy). Select as many tomatoes as you think you can eat and add a few more. Cut the ends off first so that they can cook from the top and the bottom. Place half-inch slices of them on the tray and cover each with a mixture of breadcrumbs, rosemary and thyme, lots of minced garlic and olive oil. You can put these on separately but it's easier and less messy if you mix the topping around before spreading it on the slices. Use enough oil so that the mixture clumps. Shove under the broiler in a preheated oven and in 10 minutes or so, you've got it. Be careful not to put the tray too close to the heating element — the breadcrumb mixture could carbonize before the tomatoes get warmed through.

This method is a good one for tomatoes from the "reduced-for-quick-sale"

shelf. Cut out the over-the-hill bad parts and use the rest for an economical treat.

philadelphia fried tomatoes

Before I give the impression that Americans have been out on a prolonged lunch-break in the produce department, I want to slide in a couple of Pennsylvania treats. One I still enjoy is fried tomatoes with cream gravy. Firm tomatoes are best for this — some even prefer green ones, which I do as a second choice when the frost comes and leaves us with late bloomers that never had a chance to blush.

Cut off their ends and slice the tomatoes in ⅓-inch pieces. Season them with salt and pepper. A pinch of sugar can be used too, especially if the tomatoes are not really ripe. Dip the slices in flour and fry in butter until brown on both sides (2 or 3 minutes, but not long enough for them to get mushy). Take out all but two slices of the tomatoes and keep them warm on a heated plate. Mash the slices left in the pan and add a roux made of a tablespoon each of flour and butter. When this is well dissolved, pour in ⅔ cup of milk or cream, and stir until thickened. (It will shorten your stirring time and make things run more smoothly if you pre-heat the milk.) Pour this pan gravy over the tomatoes and serve as soon as you can get it to the table. It makes a good main dish (breakfast?) or a fine complement to fried chicken and various soul foods.

Nostalgia aside, now that I'll never see first childhood again, I find the tomatoes done this way seem to be a bit on the bland side. For a livelier dish, I fry up bacon, first, and use the bacon drippings instead of butter. If the bacon is not very lean, I pour off some of the fat, add butter and proceed as above.

zucchini at its best?

We had a house-guest from Pennsylvania Dutch country who was surprised to hear us complaining about how dull zucchini often seemed to be. She donned an apron and in scant minutes, made us a dish for lunch that was and is the best I've had of this not-so-elusive vegetable. She sliced the zucchini in very thin rounds, unpeeled, and sautéed them rapidly and lightly in butter over high heat. She added freshly squeezed lemon juice, a liberal amount of chopped, fresh dill and stirred in sour cream. She left this on the heat just long enough for the cream to get warm but not long enough for the zucchini slices to turn mushy. I later found that it is still good when made with dried dill weed, but fresh is better. This is a quick, easy and delicious way to use up the zucchini you might not have wanted in the first place.

reduced for quick sale

The first fresh fruit I saw for sale in France was quite a surprise to me. I had heard so much about how particular the French were about what they ate and here were blemished pears, spotty oranges, and wrinkled plums that looked most unappetizing to my American eyes. Then I tasted and began to realize what I had been missing all my life.

From outward appearances, much of European market produce would be relegated to one of our supermarket rotten racks. It's not that they don't have the gorgeous stuff too. Paris grocers in the high rent districts have displays that would make it marvelously on Madison Avenue. The sidewalk set-up in front of Fauchon's is worth a trip to the Madeleine just to look. Everything looks as though it had escaped from the Louvre, so artistically is the perfect produce arranged to please. You have to pay dearly for these marriages of beauty and quality, but the other fifty million French who don't patronize the deluxe do insist on good-tasting food, whether or not it is beautiful to behold.

It seems that our nation's "anxiety makers" are working on our comestible sensibilities from two directions. Pride is played upon to the extent that we are conditioned to buy the freshest looking specimens, which should look as close to perfect as possible. This status prod is coupled with the fear-fostering implication that food which looks a little "off" is probably spoiled and will hurt the one who eats it.

To realize how appearances can deceive, consider the case of the orange. Many American consumers will not buy oranges unless they sport the color of the same name. Tropical travelers are reluctant, at first, to sample greenish citrus, which is mistakenly believed to indicate lack of ripeness. In order for an orange to achieve its expected color, naturally, it must undergo some cold temperature. There is chlorophyll near the surface of orange skins. The chlorophyll is kept intact by a protective membrane that is allergic to cold. When a cold snap occurs, oranges will blush in the chill. Those which are not ripe, but left on the trees after a cold spell, will turn green again. This merely points up the fact that the color is not a reliable indicator of ripeness.

Oranges that are used for frozen juice are often picked green but ripe. However, when they are sold to be "processed" at home, they have to look orange regardless of their qualities or they won't sell. Ethylene gas will turn a *ripe* green orange *orange*. It won't turn a *green* green orange, *orange*. For recalcitrant citrus, there is a Citrus Red No. 2 dye which will do the trick, but its presence is supposed to be signalled by stamping, at least in oranges from Florida.

Growers were experimenting with a spray that made beautiful skins but caused brown spots inside which were not good to look at or eat. All of this is no reason to swear off oranges. There are plenty of good ones available most of the time. Just don't insist on looks when you buy. That way, you won't miss out on the "Ugli," a Jamaican cross-breed of grapefruit, tangerine and Seville oranges that is so un-glamorous that they hung that name on it to let you know it's supposed to look like that.

There are two reasons I buy produce which is "reduced for quick sale." One is economy and the other is ripeness. When California goes under water and lettuce gets up to over a dollar a head, it just isn't worth it to me to buy it at that price. Apparently, there other others who abstain and after a crop has been in the store a few days, the boys in the back room pull off the gummy outside leaves and pack up the rest into bargain lots. I like the interiors better anyway and this way I don't feel "ripped off."

Artichokes get way up there in price too, and stay unbought. They look awful on the rotten rack. If you catch them in time, however, they are quite good enough for the artichoke freaks in our house. We strip off a few outside leaves and proceed as usual. Actually, they often look bedraggled when fresh in European markets, especially in places where it gets very hot.

I often wonder what those TV talk show cooks would talk about if they didn't spend so much time telling us to rub lemon juice over just about everything to keep colors looking fresh. Nobody likes lemons more than I do, but what a waste some of them are put to just capitalizing on their cosmetic capabilities. I almost always wait for lemons to be reduced. I have found that the longer they are kept, the more juice they furnish and, if they are not put into the refrigerator to make them last longer, they can even improve in taste. I generally buy 20 or 30 when they are cheap and squeeze most of them. The juice goes into small bottles, which are one of the few things that will fit into those funny nooks on the freezer door.

Economy aside, there's the eternal search for something ripe. Mangoes show up in our markets from time to time. Their price is usually in inverse proportion to their edibility and, beautiful as they are to look at, most of them — in their arrival state — are good only for making chutney. Chutney requires unripe mangoes for best results. After they have sat around a spell, they lose enough of their looks to qualify for the "reduced" shelf. Other mango fans know this too, so they don't last long once they get affordable. Bananas are another fruit which has to age to get good. Just about the time they are fit, they look awful. Once they start going, they shouldn't hang around long before being eaten. They are worth buying on the cheap when the regulars get up around 50 cents a pound.

Back in the "olden days," I was somewhat brainwashed by Chiquita Banana, who used to end her jingle with ". . . never, never, never, put them in the re-frige-r-ator." Granted, they look disgusting when all brown and cold, but if you have ever eaten a frozen one, you know what a good treat they can be when nearly over the hill. Put popsicle sticks in their ends and little kids will think that they are new kind of popsicle and so eat something good for themselves without knowing it.

We have several chain supermarket outlets nearby. The largest always has something worth buying at low, reduced prices. Another which has much less turnover rarely offers reductions. Much of its full-price stuff looks pretty ho-hum to begin with. I asked a clerk at one of the other large markets why they had no rotten rack. ". . . Because we have a salad bar," was his reply.

potatoes

When the *Conquistadores* went to the New World looking for gold, they found something far more valuable — potatoes. But when they took the potato back home with them to the Old World, it was not an overnight success. The French thought of potatoes as ornamental plants, which accounts for their flowery name of *pommes de terre* (apples of the earth). The more adventurous Germans plowed right in and apparently haven't quit since. Sir Walter Raleigh introduced potatoes to England, though they didn't really catch on in Ireland until close to the nineteenth century. In the meantime, the French were finally convinced that potatoes were the right stuff by Antoine Parmentier, who learned about them the hard way during a seven-year stretch as a Prussian prisoner of war. In true French-food fashion, his name has been immortalized and appears today on French menus in *potage parmentière*, a.k.a. cream of potato soup.

Two factors help explain the continuing popularity of potatoes: 1) They will grow where few other things will, from below sea level in Holland to thousands of feet up in the Andes; 2) they can be made into French fries.

Homemade French fries are so easy to make and so delicious to eat that it is a wonder to me that so many people will settle for the frozen excuses much in vogue. Ten bucks will buy a small, electric deep-fryer which will make enough for two persons in one operation. I barely made it through last summer when my grandniece, Jennie, found out I could make French fries at home. As far as she was concerned, she could have been bunking at McDonald's.

french-frying

In French-frying, temperature is important. 375 to 380 degrees is the best temperature for potatoes if you are using thin strips. Thin strips need the high heat at the beginning. Otherwise, you'll have soggy fries—the price

impatient cooks pay when they can't wait for hot enough oil to seal their outsides and keep grease from penetrating. When you remove the first batch, let the fryer heat back up. With larger-cut pieces, oil that's too hot (rare unless you have a gas stove) will produce fries that are steel-jacketed outside, raw inside. If your apparatus has no thermostat, spring for a thermometer. It will come in handy for other things once you get the skill to judge potato-frying by eye.

buying the right potatoes

Buying the right potatoes for the method you prefer to use is another matter. There are more than 5,000 varieties of potatoes and about 150 of them have been grown in the U.S. at one time or another! All of these tubers ring the changes on eight species, of which only one, *Solanum tuberosum*, is grown in the U.S., currently in about fifty varieties. How many of these you'll find in your market depends on demand, clientele, price — lots of obvious causes.

Roughly, the choice boils down to two categories — waxy or mealy. Waxy potatoes are what you want for potato salad and thick fries. They can spend more time in the lower-temperature oil without going limp on you. Mealy ones are better for baking and mashing and quick-cooking thin fries. The question is: "How do I tell the difference between the two while at the market?" To sort out those 50 + varieties would take some doing. Furthermore, the same race of potato can vary considerably according to the climate and soil where it grows. So this is only a brief starting point from which you can launch your own investigation where you live.

WAXY types. From Maine, there are Chippewas, Irish Cobblers, Katahdins and Sebagos. From Michigan, there are Chippewas and Russet Rurals. Pennsylvania, Nebraska and Wisconsin are known respectively for Katahdins, Triumphs and Sebagos. Most of the waxy types have smooth skin.

MEALY types. Idaho and Washington are the principal suppliers of Russet Burbanks, which comprise some 40 percent of our market. New York has Green Mountains. Wisconsin has Irish Cobblers (and more Sebagos). Minnesota and North Dakota have good baking potatoes (Red River Reds), but you almost have to live out there to find them. Most Russet varieties can be recognized by their rough skin, and look something like a very fine-grained cantaloupe, if there were such a thing.

For those who just want potatoes and never mind the claptrap, there's no problem. Your supermarket probably won't give you a great choice anyway. Usually, they identify potatoes by state. Asking a clerk if he has any Irish Cobblers might engender a rude response — there are a lot of Irish working in Massachusetts. We do get many Prince Edward Island potatoes around here. P.E.I.'s are the ones most often recommended in this neck of the woods and they come close to all-purpose.

I was far less particular in this matter until I discovered that potatoes can be a real treat instead of a humdrum staple. If you care to join me in the search for the ultimate spud, however, here's a kitchen trick that will give you a chuckle, amaze your friends and, incidentally, help classify any "unknown" potatoes you may encounter. It works because mealy potatoes are denser than waxy ones. Stir a tablespoon-and-a-half of salt in a cup of water and plop in a piece of the potato in question. If it floats, French fry it or use it for salad. If it doesn't, bake or mash it. I've tried this — it really does work.

Potatoes usually do not store well at home unless you've got a root cellar or cold-room. It won't make much difference which ones you buy if they have already been kept too long or improperly. Freezing makes them not only lose their nutritive values but gets you a mushy result on cooking. If they have green areas, they can be bitter, nature's way of letting you know they can be toxic! To keep the doctor away, peel any greenish spuds well beyond any green layers present. Don't buy ones that show sprouts — they are over the hill. Great big ones are frequently hollow if they are not specially grown and *selected* for baking. You can't even count on price as an indicator.

The best potatoes I have found recently, sitting next to 59-cents-a-pound beauties, were 98 cents for a 10-pound sack. They were called "Little Russes" and were probably cheap because they were so small. I like that size. They fit whole into my *mouli*. When I have a hankering for potato chips or shoestrings, that is where I put them, after scrubbing them under the faucet. One secret in making good chips is to keep them separated. By putting them through the mill held over the boiling oil, each chip falls separately and gets oiled in time to keep it from sticking to its neighbors. It is undoubtedly one of the sloppiest kitchen operations extant. You should be in a good mood when you make potato chips. But, even if you are not on top of the world when you start, you will be when you eat the first ones. Guests at our house are amazed that potato chips can be made at home and very pleased to consume them hot off the plate. Now if only they would help clean up the spattering . . .

baking potatoes

There are people who believe that potatoes are fattening per se. Not so — it depends on how they are fixed. Oil-enhanced French fries and chips will creep down to your waistline if you're not a trifle abstemious. On the other hand, a plain, baked potato will be noticed only temporarily by your scales. But alas, some cannot deal with baked potatoes unless they are buttered and disguised in sour cream and chives.

I enjoyed a supreme baked potato on a sidewalk in Granada (Spain) one crisp winter's eve. It was plucked from a charcoal-fired barrel by a little old

lady in black. she squeezed open the top, sprinkled on some salt and handed it to me in a newspaper cone in exchange for three pesetas—about a nickel at the time. It wasn't only the atmosphere that made it so good. The potato had taste, something not always allowed by modern American marketing methods.

pommes de terre souflées

For a real change of pace, try your hand at *pomme de terres soufflées*, puffed up potatoes. This is a great method to use when you want to show off, but since it can be tricky, you're better off if you practice without guests the first few times. It takes a good, firm waxy potato and two trips to the fryer. (Two fryers are better than one for this, but it can be managed with a single one.)

Peel and cut the potato into slices about an eighth of an inch thick. I suggest that you practice by cutting one potato into different width slices to see which one works the best in your kitchen. Put the potatoes in the 375 degree oil and fry five to seven minutes—when they rise to the top, they are ready to take out and drain. Then, when the oil gets hot again, even hotter than the first time if you can swing it, put them back into the oil and watch them swell up like little cream puffs.

The reason for the two fryers is twofold: you can prevent the potatoes from cooling down too long between baths and it's easier to make the second immersion hotter. But don't rush out for the second fryer unless you become a *pommes soufflées fanatique*. They *can* be done with one utensil.

josé's mashed potatoes

Mashed potatoes are not high on my list of favorites, but everyone who has them at our house flips out over the way José makes them, so I feel I should pass along his system, just in case.

First peel the spuds. Depending on how much time you have to let them cook, you can either leave very small ones whole or cut larger ones into pieces of uniform size. Sameness in size will help avoid lumps in the end result by having all potato pieces cook to the same degree at the same time. Try to time things so that they will finish cooking just before you are ready to eat. Drop them in slightly salted (optional), already boiling water and let them stay there, covered, for 20 minutes or so. I usually slide a paring knife into them to check for tenderness but José is so good at it that he can tell by just looking. Incidentally, peeled potatoes will turn dark if left exposed to the air, so either peel just before cooking or peel and store under water until boiling time.

The next step can be done by hand but it's a lot easier if you have a mixer. If you don't have a mixer, a ricer will help. The point is that you want to mash them as easily and thoroughly as possible without wearing yourself to a nub. While mashing, have a saucepan of milk warming up on the stove and some soft butter handy. Add a pinch of salt and about half a stick of butter per pound of potatoes and mix awhile. The potatoes have to be hot off the stove and drained, of course. (José puts the butter in the bowl before the potatoes and gets it good and creamy.) Then, pour in a little milk and mash away. Then **very** slowly *add more and more* hot milk and, by and by, the right moment will come for you to stop—they'll look like heavy whipped cream—so stop and serve.

leftover mashed potatoes

When José is there to fix and eat 'em, we rarely have any leftover mashed potatoes. When we do, I sometimes make my own version of potato pancakes. When properly prepared, José's potatoes are light and fluffy but they can be messy to handle, especially if you don't have a Teflon-coated pan to cook them in. (Conventional potato pancake recipes start with raw potatoes, but leftovers make even better ones in my book.) I fry up some thinly sliced and diced onions until they are golden. While that's going on, I form the potatoes into cakes two or three inches in diameter and half an inch or so thick. This will be much more successful if the potatoes have spent the night in the refrigerator. I then place the potatoes on top of the onions and flatten them down a bit with a wide spatula. The onions that aren't covered by the potatoes I scoop up and put on top of the cakes along with a few grinds from the pepper mill. After two or three minutes, I turn the cakes over and do the other sides. When top and bottom are brown and crisp, they are ready. The less you have to fiddle with them, the neater they will look, so try to get them done enough before turning the first time. They have a distinct tendency to fall apart in all directions—messy, messy, but oh so munchable.

josé's *tortilla*

While checking out the mashed method, José suggested that I mention his *tortilla española*. (N.B. A *tortilla española*—Spanish tortilla—is not the same as a Mexican *tortilla*. The Spanish make theirs with eggs as a base, while the Mexicans use cornmeal.) José's *tortilla* is guaranteed to fill up any bottomless pits you have around disguised as teenagers.

José slices raw potatoes into thin strips. If I were doing it, I would use the *mouli-julienne* but it works just as well by hand and the *tortilla* looks a little more casual. Then he pan fries the potatoes in olive oil with a dash of salt. When they are golden and done enough to eat, he pours in a couple of beaten eggs and spreads them over the potatoes. Flipped once or twice, the *tortilla* is ready to meet its maker mouth-on. Variations include green peppers and/or onions, fried before the eggs go in. Enjoy!

baked potatoes

Baking potatoes is probably the easiest way to fix them. The trouble is that it means tying up the oven for at least an hour for anything larger than a new potato. This is no problem if you are roasting something that will take that long. If you are doing a dish that takes only 10 or 15 minutes in the oven, here's a method which will get you a decent baked potato in a jiffy.

Speed things up by using a microwave oven FIRST, and then the regular oven. Give the potatoes a few minutes on high in the micro. Take them out and brush olive oil on the skins. Then put them in the other oven for the fifteen minutes the other dish requires.

With microwave only baking, what you gain in speed, you can lose in texture. For a microwaved potato to be anywhere near as good as a regular oven-baked one, it must rest with the microwaves turned off, wrapped in a towel, for as long as it takes to bake one or two. It will be better, though, if you use both ovens. Caution: no heat-conducting, metal skewers in the micro and be sure that your potato has some steam escape hatches cut into it before microwaving. Nobody likes exploding potatoes except microwave repairmen.

nicerice

One nation's potato is another nation's rice. Thanks to our heritage, we are definitely zeroed in on potatoes as a staple. For all the good reasons pointed out back in the potato section, this is a happy choice. However, literally half of the world relies on rice in the same fashion. Nine-tenths of all rice is grown in Asia where there's plenty of water and warmth to make it prosper. We grow most of ours in Mississippi, South Carolina, Texas and California.

I would not like to have to choose rice or potatoes as a favorite. To me, they are both essential. Potatoes go better with some things, rice with others. Thank God we've got both. They are both easy to prepare but, somehow, many cooks can gum up rice more easily than potatoes. There's no reason for you to do the same once you've learned how to make Nicerice.

According to a not very reliable source, WW II military pilots had two ingredients included in their survival kits to be used when forced down over unknown territory. Along with maps and C-rations, they were allotted two small flagons of spirits—one, gin; the other, dry Vermouth. When all attempts to determine his location proved fruitless, the theory went, the survivor was to begin to mix a martini. Within seconds, someone would be sure to pop out from behind a palm tree and offer advice about the proper proportions for the best drink. Chances are, if the kibitzer wasn't too addicted to his own martini version, he would also know where he and the pilot were.

Research shows that there are just as many persons who know the *only* way to cook nice rice as there are who have cornered the *original* martini formula. I hereby propose an addition to the survival kit: a ration of rice. This way, if the pilot lands next to a teetotaler, he will still have a volunteer eager to tell him the best way to cook the rice and stay sober enough to show him the way home.

Rice cooking experts are legion. They strive for perfection in two ways: dry fluffy rice whose grains do not stick to each other, and sticky rice which holds together *en masse*. Many of us who prefer the former lose sight of the fact that a large portion of the world opts for the sticky stuff because it facilitates their eating, particularly in chopstick regions. It would be difficult, to say the least, to maneuver small stir-fried goodies without little clumps of rice to help hold them together. Iberians and Middle Easterners consume great quantities of rice, too, and they tend to have their rice hang together. So, there are areas where fluffy rice might be considered a failure!

Our family goes for fluffy. For a long time, we have been using the boil and steam routine. This requires a certain amount of attention and plenty of pot and strainer manipulation. When I moved to Portugal, I discovered a rule of thumb that made the preparation easier and sometimes better. Any quantity of rice was put in a pot and covered with water a thumb's width above the top of the rice. This happened to work well for my thumbs and me but, with all the possible digital diversity and the plethora of pot diameters, there is room for error. If you are interested in trying the thumb rule, use a heavy pot. Let the rice boil vigorously for five minutes, thumb-deep under water, cover the pot *tightly* and turn off the heat. Do not even peek in the pot until fifteen minutes have gone by. If you have a cool kitchen, leave the burner on the lowest of low settings. Then, when you remove the cover, you will find *perfect* rice, especially if you have nicely proportioned thumbs.

In spite of the success I enjoyed for two decades with this method, all of my rice expertise went down the drain in early '84 when my niece revealed the ultimate, never-fail rice system, gleaned from a yellowing paperback on Oriental cookery. It is so simple, and so successful, that absolutely everyone can do it—even those who are all thumbs to begin with. Here's the way we do it now:

Take any quantity of rice, up to several cups, and toss it into a pan of boiling water. Use about 3 volumes of water to 1 of rice. Slosh it around a bit and let it boil for fifteen minutes. Then—and here's the magic part—pour in two cups of cold water and immediately drain the whole lot into a strainer. Serve as soon as possible with butter, gravy or the main dish of your choice.

Quantities are not critical, as long as you use *enough* water, i.e., more than a couple of thumbs' worth above rice level. One cup of rice will absorb approximately 2½ cups of water. If you skimp on water, you can wind up with scorched slush. On days when I am in a hurry to get back to a "MASH" re-run, I have even gotten impatient and put the rice in the water before it was bubbling. It worked fine. This could make the timing more difficult, but accuracy is not all that vital. Even after twenty minutes of hard boiling, the rice has turned out o.k. In case you leave the kitchen, keep the flame down so that the pot won't boil over. Lidded pots have a tendency to express themselves in stove-staining gurgles if you don't keep an eye on them.

You can have too little water but rarely too much for this method to work. You may waste a few vitamins and/or minerals when you discard the water, but your rice will be superb. Besides, most of the good part of the rice has already been sacrificed at the rice mill. If you are a brown rice fan, you can achieve a more nourishing result using it. Boiling time will be longer with brown rice. You should experiment with the amount of time it requires to make the rice sufficiently chewable to suit your preference.

Curiously, both the Iberian thumb and the Oriental cold water douche turn out fluffy rice, IF you use the long-grained variety, and IF you don't stir the rice while it's boiling. Much of the shorter-grained stuff, known as *Japanes*, is common in Europe. It will usually produce the gummier condition. I look for *Indian*, the longest grained that I can find on the market shelves. When I'm stuck with short-grained rice and want something a little different, I fry the rice in a little oil until it turns golden. When boiled after this treatment, it has a still different texture, with grains somewhat separated. It makes a great main dish when done up with tomatoes, peppers and onions. Fry briefly first, boil as usual and return to a frying pan with the onions and things for a final few minutes on the stove.

Since rice does not have a great deal of flavor by itself, many cooks like to perk it up by tossing a *bouquet garni* into the water. My preference, when plain rice wants a boost, is to put in saffron, which gives it a beautiful Indian yellow color and a distinctive taste. A little saffron goes a long way, which is a good thing, because it costs like smoke. I understood why it is so expensive when I saw the huge crowd of women required for a crocus harvest outside Toledo (the one in Spain). It takes the dust from the three stamens or stigmas of about a zillion crocus blossoms to make a pound of saffron—the world's most expensive spice.

In our house, we usually have a stock of little spanish penny-a-packet powders which impart a day-glo yellow to the rice without the powerful saffron taste. Such is the visual effect that the eater is liable to be persuaded that a new flavor has surfaced. Actually, it's a case of there being less there than meets the eye. Our current supply of this magic powder came from Alicante, in Spain, and its brand name is *Polluelos*. It is a by-product of corn.

Easier to find in the U.S., is *achiote*, made from *annatto* seeds, which come from a tree in the tropical parts of our hemisphere. It will accomplish a similar effect by adding both flavor and color to rice and other dishes. Check for it in a specialty spice shop if you aren't close to a Latin-American neighborhood. The *annatto* seeds are about the size of large peppercorns. To have any effect, they must be ground rather finely.

cooking under pressure

Pressure cookers became very popular in the 40's. After the novelty of fast cooking wore off, many people stuck them away in cupboards and ignored them until they wanted to can something. They are still useful for more than putting up preserves. Maybe they are destined for a new day on the range before long.

Pressure cookers came into my life in France, of all places. At the time, I found it hard to believe that renowned persnickety food-lovers would condescend to such gadgetry, but the French are practical, above all, and a pressure cooker has its place in saving time and improving some foods. They use the term *cocotte minute*, a *cocotte* being not only a lady of loose morals but also a small cooking pot with handles and a cover. There may be a connection there in the nomenclature, but French cooks from all walks of life use either at the appropriate times.

A pressure cooker depends for its usefulness on the fact that liquids boil at temperatures that increase as they come under pressure. By being confined, ingredients can be raised to higher than normal temperatures before their liquid content turns to steam. I've never been able to reconcile the opposing schools of thought about which destroys nutritive qualities more quickly— high temperatures, or prolonged exposure to heat. There is probably something to be said in favor of and against both ideas. If you've ever had to cook in Denver, though, you probably know that as the atmospheric pressure goes down, the time it takes to boil anything increases to the point where recipes have to be modified for high altitudes.

Of interest to those who get home late from work is being able to throw something tasty together in a hurry. If you like homemade soup, you can turn out a pip in short order. All you have to do is boil up vegetables of your choice for a few minutes under pressure. You can make the results into a cream soup if you wish. Just blend or process and serve. More flavor will result if you brown onions in butter first and then add the various vegetables. Stock or bouillon can be used for liquid, but plain water does quite well too. Potatoes make it hearty and creamy.

You can turn out a three-minute flan for dessert. Flan is really custard, but, by that name, it sounds fancier. One that would take three-quarters of an hour to bake in an oven will be done in a jiffy with a pressure cooker. Make a regular custard and pour it into individual cups. Cover the cups with aluminum foil. Put a half pint of water in the cooker and place the cups on a rack to keep their bottoms out of contact with the pan. After the pressure comes up and makes the valve wiggle and hiss, keep the heat on for 3 minutes. Then cool the cooker quickly and you've got flans. Cool them before serving.

Because little steam can escape, a pressure-cooker custard may come out a bit more watery on top than it would have if baked in an oven. You can fiddle around with the recipe to cut down on this but the easiest solution is to pour off the excess water when nobody's looking.

Tough meat can be quickly converted to tender pot roast under pressure. Stock from leftover bones with vegetables and spices can be made with little fuss. There are plenty of ways to use one of these cookers for meats without losing out on taste and quality. Just remember to brown meat first before you close it in for the heavy duty cooking.

There are cooks who feel uneasy about using a pressure cooker. The same people often have strong feelings about microwave ovens. Both of these pieces of hardware do have their drawbacks IF instructions are not followed. But then, your oven can blow up too, if you forget to light the gas in time. Rather than stay away in fear, approach them with *savoir-faire* and take advantage of the help they provide.

Dried beans have to be soaked for long periods to become comestible. They can be dealt with in far less time under pressure. But don't mess with any pressure cooker until you have read the directions that come with the model you are using. They will remind you not to fill the cooker over two-thirds full, or, half-full of anything that swells up in water, such as those beans or rice. Foodstuffs like split green peas which "disintegrate" while cooking are to be avoided completely when using a pressure cooker. They can play havoc with escape valves. REPEAT — read directions first.

6 | **seasonings & spices**

Three basic necessities of mine *NOW*, are garlic, olive oil and herbs. I did not grow up with them intimately except for a few things like parsley and mint. My reflections on these late-found essentials date from my second quarter-century. My nostalgia has been a long time building but I haven't stopped adding to it. Chances are that persons of more recent vintage were exposed to these basics earlier on. Whether or not you are already fellow fans, I may have something new for you, so here goes.

EAT GARLIC BUT DON'T TELL ANYONE

That's a bumper sticker from Gilroy, CA that I first saw on a Santa Cruz refrigerator door. The advice is from Gilroy, "The Garlic Capital of the World."

I didn't dwell further on Gilroy at the time, but I was soon to experience it for myself. On my way back to San Francisco from Santa Cruz, I detoured along an inner highway to admire the countryside. I was tooling along, not thinking about much of anything, when I got the distinct impression that the electrical system in my borrowed wagon was about to self-destruct. I stopped, got out and checked under the hood for the source of the peculiar smell which had alerted me. Everything looked o.k. I thought that maybe the brakes had locked temporarily. Finding nothing amiss, I got back in and drove on.

Fifteen heady moments later, the smell and I were in Gilroy. Gilroy has to be inhaled to be believed. Even with a head cold, you will sense it if you drive within 9 miles of the place from any direction, even with your windows rolled up. There is no upwind where Gilroy garlic is concerned . . . it's just there, all 16,000 acres of it. The garlic that doesn't grow within the city limits gets funneled through Gilroy on its way to the rest of the world, foisting pheromones on garlic lovers lucky enough to take Route 101, 30 miles south of San José, which is just a hop, skip and a jump south of San Francisco.

Garlic has been the subject of overkill in the U.S. When glossy magazines run out of sex articles, they push garlic, which, incidentally, has long been considered to have aphrodisiac properties—*as long as both parties partake.* When it comes to health magazines, garlic is right up there with ginseng as a preventative for everything from high blood-pressure to virus invasion. I enjoy garlic for its taste and am delighted that I am benefiting from all these side-effects, regardless of their authenticity.

I really got to know garlic when I went to live in France. My first trip to the local grocer in Roussillon, a tiny village in the Vaucluse, clued me in vividly. I soon learned how important this tasty plant is to that segment of the population whose enjoyment of the table comes first in life. A neighbor had put two kilos in her shopping net and I asked if she were laying in supplies

INDUSTRIAL GARLIC PRESS - self-cleaning!

for the winter. It turned out to be a week's worth, no more. I got the message and have been acknowledging it ever since with one sense or another. One of the great pleasures of traveling is that once I leave the land of tooth-paste and mouth-wash, the hand-over-mouth gesture becomes superfluous in most other civilizations. Garlic fumes being ubiquitous — defenses become superfluous.

If asked for my one favorite dish that depends on garlic, I wouldn't hesitate to talk about the *pollo al ajillo* I already raved about a while back. If it and a few of the other garlicky formulas described have made your taste buds rise up and beg for more, you should become acquainted with Gilroy.

When I went through the town, I paused long enough to pick up a dynamite collection of recipes and garlic lore on the spot. They are in a book put out by the Gilroy Garlic Festival Association, Inc. You won't have to go all the way to get your copy. They'll send you one for $7.95 (paperback) or $10.95 for one with plastic spiral binding. Add on $1.50 for postage and handling and send your check to:

GILROY GARLIC FESTIVAL
P.O. Box 2311
Gilroy, CA 95020

They will send you the 2nd edition of "THE GARLIC LOVERS COOK BOOK." It has over 220 garlic recipes! In 1985, they had already sold in the neighborhood of 200,000 copies. When they add the next bunch of recipes, the price may go up, so send for your copy now.

olive oil

Some of the most agreeable moments of my life have been spent in olive country. I've missed out on Greece and the Middle East, but my exposure to the delights of the olive in Europe have been sufficient to make me a life-long aficionado of this magnificent fruit and its glorious essence. If God has invented many other things better than olive oil to convert casual cooks to master chefs, he has kept them to himself. Administered in *discreet* quantities, olive oil *can* transform a mundane effort into a succulent dish fit for the most refined of eaters.

Olive oil is not always immediately likeable to those who didn't get their first samples with their mother's milk. It runs a taste gamut from fruity through neutral to rancid. What constitutes rancid to some inexperienced palates is not necessarily a reflection of the actual state of the oil — some of the industrial strength stuff may be simply a bit too fully flavored for non-habitués.

Etymologists enjoy the capricious terms used to define olive oil quality. Serious buyers should be familiar with these. *Virgin* oil comes as is from the first pressing of the olives. The second pressing has a tendency to coax out rougher flavors from the fruit and when combined with "virgin" first pressings, the result still qualifies as *pure*. If the taste is too pronounced, refining is called for to reduce the amount of oleic acid. The percentage of this acid determines the label. Virgin oil can contain up to 4 percent of oleic acid, but there are at least three more categories: *fine, superfine,* and *extra virgin*, which are limited to 3, 1.5, and 1 percent oleic acid. Sometimes, labels will have *pure* and something like *super-fine*, thus leaving the buyer in the dark and obliged to buy and sample in order to know what's in the can. If the oil you find is in a bottle, you can often anticipate its strength of flavor by the color. The eyeball-rule is: the greener the oil, the more taste it will have.

The above terms are used by the Spanish, French and Italians. Oil produced in the U.S. has to abide by stricter qualifications. "Virgin olive oil" must result from the first pressing without any other processing. Further refinement and blending call for the label of "pure olive oil."

In production, Spain could be considered the General Motors of olive oil; France, the Peugeot; Italy, the Alfa Romeo; and Portugal, the Rolls Royce, or Edsel, depending on your reaction to the really real thing. For those who want olive oil but not the olive taste, the Spanish have succeeded in refining their wonderful base product to such an extent that sometimes its flavor no longer divulges its ancestry. Some of it could be pure Wesson as far as taste goes. The French, as usual, have a most exquisite product, but their top-of-the-line stuff goes for up to $20 a quart in the U.S. and that outlay is ridiculous except as a status symbol. The Italians have superb oil but you almost have to make a trip to Italy to acquire it. They are understandably so fond of the good stuff that they tend to keep it for themselves.

It is curious how some of us food-nuts can shell out big bucks for a bottle of fine wine without having a nervous breakdown but balk at expensive oil. Especially when we consider that the wine is gone with the meal but a quart of super-duper olive oil can be nursed along for weeks.

Medium-priced Italian olive oil is the safest to use if you want to combine tempting taste with a modicum of economy. When you really get hooked,

Portuguese is the ultimate. Like Rolls Royces, Portuguese olive oils are *not* for everyone. Therefore, do not start in with them even if you are fortunate enough to have a source of supply. There's no turning back once you get hooked on its powerful pungency. A better bet, especially if you are cooking for more than one, is to start with Spanish, which can be so mild that it will slip into your daily dishes without arousing notice until the hook has been set. Also, Spanish oil is the least expensive — we pay less for it than the Spanish do, a hard, unpleasant economic fact for the altruistic, but one which we'd do well to take advantage of nevertheless.

Our household has strong auxiliary Iberian roots. For one, I have spent much time in Spain, and in Portugal where I bought a house in the early 60s. For another, we have a resident Spaniard, José, who came from Córdoba to live with us a dozen years ago. Between us, we keep the demand for olive oil and olives at a reasonable peak. For cooking, we generally blend one quart of *Saloio*, a Portuguese oil available in this area, with whatever other olive oil is available in the supermarket at around ten dollars a gallon. This way we enjoy a pronounced olive taste that won't send visiting ingenuous oil-samplers running for the Lavoris. In all honesty, cooking with such strong oil, un-cut, can make the kitchen (and much of the rest of the house) smell a lot like a back alley in a Portuguese fishing village. While I prefer that kind of aroma to Air-wick, not everyone does.

We do use *Saloio* straight for salads where it is most welcome. Cooking with the tastiest olive oil can not only be a strain on the nose but can also be a waste. Once olive oil gets heated past 140 degrees, it begins to change flavor and not always for the better! Olive oil isn't improved at the other end of the temperature scale either. Keep it out of a hot place but avoid the temptation to put it in the refrigerator. Store it in the tin or glass it comes in. Avoid copper or iron for storage, but stainless steel is o.k. Keep it out of plastic containers, too, as some plastic material can interfere with its taste.

My section of the country is home to a large Portuguese population so I have little trouble locating the oil of my dreams. If you live outside of Massachusetts, Rhode Island or Connecticut, you may have a problem finding Portuguese products. In that case, I suggest writing to Mr. José Gouveia, Jr., P.O. Box N-1086, New Bedford, MA 02746. Mr. Gouveia is the proprietor of the import firm bearing his name. He will be delighted to tell you where you might obtain not only *Saloio* but dozens of other products from "ethnic" herbs to tinned sardines. He is a wholesaler, only, so you won't be able to get individual shipments from him.

olive lore

Historians say that the Egyptians were enjoying the olive and its juices 3000 years B.C. They used the first pressing for food, the second for cosmetic

purposes, and whatever they could squeeze out after that, they put in their lamps and stoves. The heady atmosphere generated by all of these olive by-products is still one of the distinct features of Mediterranean travel today. It can come as a shock. I remember vividly my first harvest-time drive through *La Carmona*, a town nestled in olive orchards between Seville and Cordóba in Spain. The experience was akin to first sniffing into Marcus Hook, PA, whose petroleum refinery appurtenances call for closed windows and clothespins for all but the hardiest noses.

Even though an olive oil atmosphere is easier to become accustomed to and a lot more pleasant, it tends towards raunchy around pressing time. After I had spent some time in olive country, I found that I missed the aroma when

I came home. I also miss the street-vendors who sell olives for pittances out of barrel-laden carts the way we peddle hot dogs over here.

Not everyone will enjoy the odoriferousness of "olive country," but gentle incursion of the olive into everyday cuisine will be appreciated by most persons if the introduction is not too abrupt. If need be, you can always smuggle it in accompanying garlic, which is even harder for some to fall in love with. Maybe a drive through Gilroy with a flask of olive oil in your glove compartment would get your friends and family saturated beyond the point of no return. Shucks, in spite of not knowing either item until I was 26, I can't live without them now.

about eating olives

There are basically two categories of olives available to us in the U.S. There are the little green ones, sometimes whole, sometimes stuffed with pimientos or almonds. These we find on appetizer trays and at the bottom of Martinis. Then there are the Deli models which go from green to black and often have herbs to enhance their flavor. Almost all commercially prepared olives, especially the small green ones, are loaded with salt which keeps them from spoiling but spoils their appeal, at least in our house. We usually wash them with water, add vinegar, oregano, rosemary, thyme and a few lashings of garlic. After they have lounged around a day or two in this new environment, they have become transformed to conform to our desires.

I've never met a likeable California black olive. I believe that it must be because of the treatment they undergo once picked. Apparently they are first dipped in a ferrous gluconate solution, then into lye, then put in brine and, eventually, sterilized—a tough cycle for anything to undergo. I have even sampled home-cured black olives at a lovely hacienda on Whiskey Hill in California—in spite of the inspiring surroundings, which included a panorama of the olive trees against the Pacific, the olives were bland and unappetizing.

Greek olives are picked in various stages of ripeness and packed in salt or brine — no lye. Spain cures many olives this way too. With the herb and vinegar treatment, these become our favorites. Portuguese olives are usually on the bitter side for those used to Spanish and Greek varieties.

The element that the lye removes, oleuropein, is very bitter and doubtless makes the Portuguese olives less than palatable to many. Somehow, even when the Greeks skip the lye, their pickling cancels out much of the oleuropein flavor. As for the little green pimentoed olives, they are picked before they are ripe, subjected to lye and then brined. Getting them stuffed and placed artistically in jars occupies many nimble fingers in Spain, where most of them originate. In fact, all but 2 or 3 percent of the world's olives are grown around the Mediterranean (including Portugal, in spite of its being on the Atlantic).

My feelings are so intense about the proper olive that I once abandoned forever an Italian restaurant in the North End of Boston (the Italian section). Though the restaurant is across the street from a grocery store where they sell old-country olives out of barrels, they had the temerity to put California black ones in my salad.

salads

All but the most refined Spanish oil will announce its presence when it's sprinkled onto salad. Plain old lettuce with oil and vinegar does much more for me than any of the bottled concoctions masquerading as salad dressings, no matter what they are used to cover. When traveling by air, I always try to take along little bottles of olive oil and vinegar to perfume plasticized fare; they not only help out the tired lettuce but other dishes as well. With my emergency kit, which also includes a pocket pepper grinder, I'm ready to make my food fly as high as the plane.

cooking

Almost anything that starts with a dab of butter in the pan will be helped out by adding a shot of olive oil at the start. The dairy industry has succeeded in removing most of the taste from our commercial butter, replacing it with water. While standard butter is heating, it has to get hot enough to evaporate this water and the addition of oil will not only help to keep the butter from burning but will also improve the taste.

If you can't stand the thought of olive oil in your butter, other cooking oils will do the same, and if you are using the "other" spread, well, you're in the wrong book. Seriously, if you rub cuts of meat with olive oil before braising,

broiling or roasting, they will taste much better when done. Unless you are using Portuguese oil, very few persons will be able to identify the source of the improved meat flavor.

Olive oil works wonders with French-fried potatoes and makes potato chips sublime. Until I hit the lottery for the big payoff, I'll have to wait for a return to Spain for deep olive-oil frying. There, where olive oil is a necessity rather than a luxury, there are people out frying chips and *churros* in squares and open markets all over the country from the crack of dawn. *Churros* are simply fried dough. *Churro* vendors fill up large syringes with thick batter and inject it into vats of boiling oil to form long segments or rings. Spaniards enjoy these with coffee, much as we delight in dunking doughnuts. *Churros* are not sweet, however. I find them tastier with sugar sprinkled on them, but then I take my coffee straight.

A Portuguese habit I've never been able to kick is a dish of potatoes, boiled, drained and served with olive oil and vinegar. The Portuguese serve potatoes, in one form or another, with most fish dishes. When the spuds are presented boiled, the custom is to mash them up a bit with olive oil and vinegar, cruets of which are always on their tables. Even American kids dig this version. Try it; they'll like it. I've known it to snuff out incipient anorexia in a few recalcitrant teen-aged non-eaters, if you can fathom such an oxymoron.

There is a marvelous sweet cake called *Pão-de-Ló*. It's made with olive oil and honey, among other things! You'll find it further on under desserts.

herbs and spices

Early settlers in our country were definitely gung-ho on herbs and spices. History books are still trying to make us believe that the Pilgrims came here to escape religious persecution and that the conquistadores were primarily on the prowl for gold. That was only part of it. They were also looking for something interesting to eat. So were a lot of other explorers. They did find freedom and gold but they also modified their European diets in many ways. Initially, however, herbs and spices were the important objects to be sought, acquired and used.

In the early 1900s, interest in natural seasonings (and medicines) died down in many parts of our country. Why this happened is a book in itself. What concerns us here is not why they fell from favor, but how to take advantage of their coming back into flavor.

And not a minute too soon. If modern agriculture succeeds in removing much more taste from what it grows, we might just as well start eating the packaging.

Herbs are usually mentioned in the same breath as spices. There is a distinction between the two. Herbs are leaves and soft stems of plants, most of which can be grown in temperate climates. Spices are buds, bark, flowers, seeds, and roots or fruits of trees and plants. Most of them grow in the tropics and consequently, when used by us, are dried in form.

flavoring versus seasoning

Herbs and spices are used to flavor or season foodstuffs. Seasoning enhances the taste of a dish without altering its basic flavor. Flavoring imparts a taste of its own. If seasoning is overdone, it becomes flavoring, which is not always for the better. The proper use of either is a measure of the skill of the cook.

For example, oregano in a spaghetti sauce, used in moderation at the inception of sauce making, imparts a flavor we recognize, a seasoning that's "Italian." If it's dumped on a plate of spaghetti at serving time, we're hit in the chops with a flavor that's oregano over everything else. Unless the eater is a real oregano freak, this can be a disappointment.

When to add herbs and spices to any dish is important. As a rule, whole spices—like peppercorns or cloves—should go in at the beginning, because it takes awhile to extract their full flavor. Ground pepper or cloves dissipate their strength more rapidly, so you might be better off adding them later in something like a long simmering stew. Actually, the taste of some herbs and spices change during cooking. This is why it is often recommended to "adjust" the seasoning near the end of cooking something. If the same flavoring is added at different times throughout a preparation, you may be able to benefit from more than one good effect. The semantics of seasoning and flavoring seem to overlap here—indeed, their effects in cooking do too.

dried versus fresh

Properly used dried or fresh herbs will perk up your life and embellish your reputation. If you are accustomed to using them, you already know that a *little goes a long way*, especially those that are dried. Dried herbs lack the delicacy of fresh ones and their decreased volume might lead us to think they aren't strong. In fact, some are stronger. Dry oregano, for example, is more potent than fresh measure for measure.

Age is not always as critical as we have been told for all spices and herbs. While they do fall off in strength, many retain sufficient goodness to be useful. The amount may have to be increased, but not much. We have a jar of *Epice Aromatique* bought from Fortnum & Mason in 1937. These peppercorns and other spices still have enough flavor left to perform satisfactorily, even in moderation. A bag of *Herbes de Provence* bought in Guadeloupe, although only 5 years old, also comes in handily and tastily on occasion.

For a recent Christmas, we bought a bay wreath for the front door. Not only did it dress up the house but around mid-January, it began a new life. A half dozen little bags of leaves wound up at our bridge club to delight the members. Julia Child always recommends "imported" bay leaves, but domestic ones are not all that bad. They are slightly different in flavor but acceptable for many purposes.

A guest chef got carried away by the availability of so many bay leaves from our wreath. A Virginia ham we were fixing almost bit the dust when he dropped eleven (dry) bay leaves into the ham brew! Fortunately, they were retrieved before they had a chance to unleash their power. One bay leaf is usually enough for a whole stew and two or three provide plenty of punch for a ham! When in doubt, use any herb or spice sparingly until you are well acquainted with its effects. Leave bay leaves and any other leafy herbs whole until they go into the pot. Last-minute crumbling keeps the pungency sealed in until it is needed.

It is important to remember that more is not necessarily better. Too much of one herb can successfully annihilate a *pièce de résistance* and a mixture of too many different herbs will not only cancel each other out but can also drown out the main ingredient and turn a promising stew into cough medicine!

There's much more to be said about herbs and spices and a chart seems a good way to prune some verbiage for those who want uncluttered information. Here then is a compendium of classic combinations in culinary composition.

chart of herbs and spices

SEASONING	FRESH	DRY	WHOLE	GROUND	FREEZABLE FORM	BOUQUET GARNI	PICKLING	MARINADES	EGGS	SALADS	SAUCES	STOCKS	SOUPS	CHEESE DISHES	VEGETABLES	FISH	MEATS	DESSERTS	FLAVOR/USAGE
allspice	•	•	•		brown berry												braised sausages	pies stewed fruit	tastes of cloves, nutmeg, & cinnamon
basil	•	•	•		leaves, crushed or whole			•							peas, squash, eggplant		lamb		popular in Italian cuisine
bay leaf	•	•	•		leaves powdered	•	•					•					braised stews		very potent
cayenne (red pepper)	•	•	•		bright red powder						•		•	•		•	•		looks like paprika; but is very hot
celery seed			•		usually ground often with salt				•		•		esp. jellied		tomatoes	•			from plant similar to but not celery
chili powder	•		•		blend of cumin, garlic, hot pepper, oregano			•									ground		Mexican dishes
chives	•	•		•	looks like hollow grass			•	•	•	•		•	•	•	•	ham		like mild onions best fresh
cinnamon		•	•		bark from cinnamon or cassia tree		•											yes many	good for flavoring drinks
cloves	•	•	•		dried flower buds			•			•	•				esp. creole	ham, braised meat		
coriander (dried)	•	•	•		hollow light brown seed			•									pork, hot dog ingredient	gingerbread	dried vastly different from fresh

SEASONING	FRESH	DRY	WHOLE	GROUND	FREEZABLE / FORM	BOUQUET GARNI	PICKLING	MARINADES	EGGS	SALADS / SAUCES	STOCKS	SOUPS	CHEESE DISHES	VEGETABLES	FISH	MEATS	DESSERTS	FLAVOR/USAGE
coriander (fresh)	•				aka. Chinese parsley cilantro – coentros			•		•			•					popular in Mexican cuisine
cumin		•	•	•	small seed ground			•		•				sauerkraut	in Portugal esp. •	sausage esp. Spanish & Portuguese		Mediter. cooking salient spice in curry
curry	•	•	•	•	ground yellowish powder			•		•		•			•	•		mild to hot
dill	•	•	•	•	fresh sprigs seeds & weed		•		•	•		garnish	•		•			northern European specialty
fennel	•	•		•	plant like celery or seeds				•	•	•	•	•		•			eaten fresh as dish or as herb
ginger	•	•	•		fresh (grated or sliced) crystallized		•	•		•			•		•	•	•	good pickled in vinegar or wine
juniper berries		•			dark berries			•						sauerkraut		game		makes gin "gin"
mace	•		•		skin of nutmeg				•			esp. chicken				•	•	milder than nutmeg but similar
majoram	•			•	crushed leaves	•										pâtés lamb poultry		like oregano but much milder
mint	•	•	•	•	leaves				•	•		•		peas, potatoes		lamb	used for tea and with fruit juices	comes in spear- & peppermint

Spice	Form	Notes
mustard	dry powder or wet	large variety of "flavored" mustards available
nutmeg	seed of nutmeg fruit	strong flavor
oregano	leaves, whole or powdered	popular in Mediterranean food
paprika (Spanish)	ground sweet red pepper	mild – used greatly for color
paprika (Hungarian)	darker red pepper	strong flavor, tends to be "hot"
parsley	leaves curly or flat-flakes	flat (Italian type) better for cooking
pepper	black or white	pepper flavor
pepper (red – hot)	fresh or dried	used when you need pepper flavor plus HEAT
rosemary	sprigs of needles – crushed	should be crumbled if it is to be left in finished dish
sage	green fuzzy leaves	
saffron	stigma of crocus	very strong & expensive
savory (summer & winter)	leaves crushed	"summer" savory preferred pungent flavor
tarragon	narrow green leaves	good flavoring for vinegar
thyme	small green leaves	very widely used

Additional column labels appearing in the usage chart: "many meats", "chicken veal", "lamb chicken pork", "poultry pork sausages", "chicken & veal esp.", "beans & tomatoes", "cream" sauces, "French dressing", "garnish", "seeds", "esp. French", "most widely used herb for flavor and/or garnish", "most widely used spice".

curry

The use of herbs and spices reaches a peak in the composition of curry. In pre-refrigeration days, cooks devised various combinations of very spicy condiments to preserve foods subject to deteriorization in tropical climates. Most of these concoctions are powerful enough to disguise unpleasant tastes when the produce or meats go "off." Whether considered a preventative or a cure, curry is addictive. Once one acquires a taste for it, no technical excuses are required to call for using it. Curry becomes just another good way to season dishes of almost any kind.

Curry is a bit like obscenity—no one can define it, exactly, but everyone knows it when it turns up. The fact that it's often thought of as a tropical way to disguise spoilage can hardly explain why "meatless" *tons* of it are consumed by Indians who are primarily vegetarians. There is no question that it can cover a multitude of culinary sins, because it has a very strong flavor that can overpower unsavory basic foodstuffs. On the other hand, it has a delicious taste and used properly will still allow other tastes to filter through. While there are nearly as many curry formulas as there are Indian cooks, there are some basic ingredients which more or less constitute curry and differentiate it from other ethnic powders such as chili and *adobo*.

Among the ingredients which make up curry are the following: anise buds, cardamom, coriander, cumin, cloves, cassia buds, cinnamon, chili seeds, fennel seeds, garlic, ginger, mustard seeds, mace, nutmeg, pepper, saffron, salt, tamarind, turmeric and fenugreek. (I saved the fenugreek for last because I thought you might like to know that its intriguing name means "Greek hay.")

With the possible permutations and combinations of these materials, you come up with more different curries than the national debt has billions. In spite of the possibilities, there is an underlying sameness that does identify the end-result as curry. I have narrowed it down to cumin, whose scent always seems to be present in commercial curries. Though it is not difficult to make at home, I usually buy my curry powder. Even our local health store has a few. I've found something to recommend in almost all I've tried. The only one that has disappointed me so far was a batch I bought from a charming Creole crone at the outdoor market in Point à Pitre (Guadeloupe). The flavor was fine but it was gritty, due I believe to the grilled, powdered rice thrifty Creoles sometimes add to stretch out their *poudre de colombo*. It appears that when they can't think of any other way to prepare things in the Caribbean, they curry them. They offer everything from curried agouti to toucans, but I still prefer pork.

real bread coming up!

bread and mayonnaise

I don't buy skim milk, mayonnaise or ordinary bread. It's tough to get this across to house-guests who somehow feel they are doing the household a favor when they go out shopping. It's almost axiomatic that after a few days' stay, well-meaning guests will have stuffed the refrigerator with blue milk and one of those heavily advertised brands of salad dressing, which they intend to slather on sandwiches of the sliced stuff that passes for supermarket staff-of-life. If only they would eat it all before they leave.

The problem is that once they have done chipping-in "duty," they go through our real milk, the homemade mayo and the "real" bread I drive 70 miles to buy from Signor Umberto—he runs a bakery way up in the Italian section of Boston. Even the cats turn up their whiskers at the skim milk and, as for the bread, guests zero in on the crusty good stuff like locusts and leave behind the factory junk when they go. Most of the food the guests leave behind I'm too particular to eat and too cheap to throw out. Now there's a dilemma.

Regular milk is not what it used to be, but it beats the watered-down low-fat version. If I had to drink it for diet reasons, I'd give up moo-juice altogether. I remember the days when milk had cream on top. It's still available at our health food store. I bought it for a while, but they switched to plastic bottles so I went back to white wine.

Now that I've gotten that off my chest, let's get down to what I really want to tell you about: something to put on the slices. It's amazing how simple it is to make *good* mayonnaise. You'll need oil, eggs, mustard, vinegar, salt, lemon juice, and Worcestershire sauce. The last two items are optional, except for me. An egg beater or electric mixer will make this production easier, but I have done it with a fork on a plate and it wasn't all that difficult.

making the mayo

Put egg yolks in your egg beater bowl and start beating. Use the wire whip if you have a choice of beaters and work up to high speed, which gives you a better chance of emulsifying and makes a stiffer mayonnaise. Add salt and vinegar. When they are mixed in, slowly add the oil drip by drip until it catches. Then you can pour faster, but remember not to add more at one time than is already in the bowl. After you have enough oil to prove that your mayonnaise is going to "take," add the dry mustard and the Worcestershire, if you like it. Add more oil and take a taste to check for seasoning. After you've added all the oil you intend to use, add lemon juice and sample it again. When the taste suits you, you can beat in a couple of tablespoons of boiling water, which will help it stay set. Now, all you have to do is hide it from the guests.

The biggest problem is to keep the mayonnaise from turning—that is, separating—once it has started to take. You can cut down the chances of this happening by following a few basic rules: have the ingredients at the same temperature—add oil slowly and beat at high speed. If you haven't gotten the eggs out of the refrigerator in time for them to warm up, you can soon solve that by first beating them alone. Proportions of eggs to oil are flexible and depend on the weather, the size of your eggs, and your personal taste and cholesterol count. Try, however, to limit yourself to 2 or 3 ounces of oil per average yolk.

The boiling water is not absolutely necessary, but it will help the mayonnaise hang in there, especially if you are going to store it for a while. This mayonnaise would keep for weeks in the fridge if it weren't so damned delicious.

Unless I have to make an emergency batch in the blender, I use egg yolks only and save the whites for Angel food (cakes) and meringues. Including the egg white facilitates the blender method. Yolks alone are liable to firm up so fast that the blade spins furiously but no longer blends. There is a pronounced difference in taste when the white goes in—folks who like yolks prefer them alone and I'm one of those folks.

When you want to make a smaller quantity in a hurry, do this: use two whole eggs, and about half the rest of the ingredients for the regular mayonnaise formula. Put the eggs, salt, mustard and vinegar in the blender all at once. As soon as they get blurred, bring on the oil. It will make a lot of racket. The oil takes a few seconds to catch and when it does, the mixture can get so stiff that it won't move up and down in the blender. You can add vinegar to thin it down. Then, you can add more oil to make the quantity you desire. Keep a rubber spatula handy to assist the combining. I have a chewed up spatula for this purpose and it bears the wounds of previous encounters with the blender blades. Remove the rubber chips from the mayo in case you get careless. A food processor avoids some blender problems and can make a dynamite mayonnaise. If you can manage it without using any egg white, it will taste as good as it looks.

IF by some unfortunate fluke your mayonnaise separates, don't throw it out. Start with another egg yolk or two and a little salt. Beat them up as before and add just enough oil to catch. (This will work in either the regular beater or the blender, but use a clean recipient.) Then slowly pour in the disaster. It will work. It may take a while to get the knack of it. I once used eleven eggs to save the first six, but I'm not one to be discouraged easily. Besides, I was in France and couldn't bear to let the French think an American couldn't perform this simple task. I have since learned that one trouble was that the eggs were too fresh. I've heard tell that superfresh eggs will sometimes refuse to catch under any circumstances. Alas, I can no longer go out to the back yard to pick them up, as I could in those long ago days.

Once you've gotten hooked on homemade mayonnaise—and you will be—you'll have to look into ways to use up the left-over egg whites. No problem . . . Rejoin me up in the dessert section and check out meringues.

aunt bertha's american french dressing

Something we use a lot of in America, that they don't have in France, is French dressing. Like English muffins and Danish pastry, we've borrowed a remotely-related name and tacked it onto our own invention. Unless they've imported it from us, the French make a dressing that is oil and vinegar, salt and pepper, and maybe an herb or two mixed at eating time—in other words, vinaigrette. Our oleaginous, orange-colored salad dressing, the kind the house-guests leave with the skim milk, would make the average Frenchman pass on the salad course.

My tastes are eclectic, though, and there is a "day-gloish" dressing that I really dig, on occasion. To show you how broad-minded I am, I'm going to give you, direct from southern Virginia, Aunt Bertha's recipe for French dressing. I like it very much. I don't care for it on plain lettuce, which, to me, becomes the ultimate salad when simply subjected to oil and vinegar and little else. Don't knock Aunt Bertha's, though, until you've tried it. It'll save you money and it's a million times better than anything by the same-sounding name in the supermarket.

There aren't any secret ingredients — at least there won't be after you see these. The dressing contains onion, paprika, dry mustard, salad oil, tarragon vinegar, powdered sugar, cayenne pepper, salt and cider vinegar. Blend and store in the warmest part of your refrigerator. Shake (the dressing) before using.

Tarragon vinegar is available ready-made if you don't care to whip up your own. For oil, I use Wesson, but the choice is up to you. Just don't use olive oil in this. If you want to put in one egg white, it will help keep the dressing from separating but it sometimes makes it too thick to pour when it has spent time in the refrigerator. A wide-necked storage bottle is advisable. Then, if it gets too thick, you can spoon it out.

One salad this really does a job on is avocado-grapefruit. Slice an avocado, section a grapefruit, add slivers of red pimiento and combine the lot on shredded lettuce. Douse liberally with Aunt Bertha's potion cut with some of that dynamite homemade mayonnaise. I usually add a bit more vinegar on the salad but, then, I love vinegar. Use Iceberg lettuce. This is one case where its crispness provides such good texture contrast with other elements of a salad that I prefer to use it in place of one of the floppy kinds with taste.

Aunt Bertha's American French dressing makes an irresistible onion sandwich. Not everyone is equipped to handle uncooked onions, but if you are, you've got a real treat in store. Slice mild onions in thin rings and marinate them in your homemade French dressing. The longer you can leave them, the less sharp they will become — up to a point. But in as little as five minutes, the time it will take you to slice some bread and spread it with the above-mentioned mayo, they can be used. Scatter the rings on half the bread slices, sprinkle some dried dill leaves, cover with the other half of the bread and you've got yourself the ultimate sandwich. My mother makes them, along with her cucumber and her tomato sandwiches, for the bi-weekly bridge bashes. The ladies go through the onion jobs like two-legged vacuum cleaners.

Onion sandwiches are good even when regular supermarket bread is used. Get "thin-sliced" and plan to leave it out of its wrapper to dry a day ahead. It will make a better vehicle for the juicy onions.

At the Santa Cruz branch of the University of California there is a farm. On that farm, there are students who learn about agriculture by growing acres of fruits, vegetables, flowers and herbs. Their produce is filtered into local households from a farm stand, womaned in part by local gourmets who think of ways to turn a profit to the benefit of the project. One of their solutions is fancy vinegars, flavored only by herbs grown on the spot. My Santa Cruz hostess (the one with the garlic bumper sticker on her refrigerator) inspired me to look into the vinegar world. This is one reason why vinegar pops up frequently in this book. In fact, here's a bit about it.

vinegar

A triple-threat item on most kitchen shelves is vinegar of one kind or another. As foodstuff, it serves as seasoning, preservative and tenderizer. It can even be used to clean mineral deposits inside coffee-makers by cycling through a cup from time to time. In fact, it's hard to imagine life without it.

Vinegar has been around as long as wine. This is not surprising since the word vinegar comes from *vinaigre* which is French for sour wine. Vinegar is, of course, older than French but its former nomenclature remains a bit misty. It doesn't have to come from wine. For example, beer and ale which have gone beyond the pale wind up as *malt* vinegar or *alegar*. The English have more barley than grapes so they make a lot of malt vinegar. For fish-and-chips fans, it's the *only* vinegar for that particular dish. I find it a good stand-in for lemon juice, occasionally. Over-the-hill apple juice becomes cider vinegar, very common in the U.S. Vinegar was originally only a by-product but now occupies such an important place in our diet that it is no longer simply a left-over but the primary product of a thriving industry.

Vinegar comes in various concentrations of acidity and 5 percent is more or less the standard strength we are used to in this country. This degree of acidity might not have been enough for Cleopatra to dissolve Marc Antony's pearl, probably the silliest thing that's ever been done with such a useful product. Acidity strength is sometimes indicated in grains, at 10 grains to one percent. A 50 grain vinegar would be the standard 5 percent.

the simple salad

We probably use vinegar more in salads than anywhere else. Combined with oil and a dash of salt, it becomes a basic vinaigrette. Many prefer to add pepper, herbs and possibly minced onions. My preference is for the first three ingredients alone and applied in the way I learned at the southern French farm I lived on back in the '50's. There the unvarying evening ritual was carried out by *Papa*, whose principal contributions to any meal were making the sign of the cross on the loaf of bread before *he* sliced it for one and all, and mixing the salad.

Salad was invariably the penultimate course and there was always a glass bowl of freshly washed and dried lettuce leaves on the sideboard waiting its turn. One of the children would rise to get the bowl, pass it to *Papa* with a large spoon and fork and then sit back down. *Papa* would pour two or three spoonfuls of oil over the leaves and toss them lightly. He then dissolved some salt in a spoonful of vinegar, which he dribbled over the oil-covered leaves. (The reason many people are so particular in drying the leaves is that this ensures that the oil will coat them and not run down to the bottom of the bowl.) In subsequent tossing, the vinegar married•the oil and further distributed the flavor throughout the salad. Curiously, *Papa* did not even add garlic, which, in that part of the country, goes into almost everything but ice cream.

This method is easy and good but perhaps too simple for some who do not consider the salad as a necessary part of the evening meal. Such a low key approach to salad is analogous (for many French) to drinking ordinary wine whenever they eat. For us, both salads and wines tend to be featured items that don't appear at every sitting. Considering some of the bottled dressings and bargain wines some people resort to, it's probably just as well.

flavored vinegars

As tasty as it is straight, there's no reason why you can't enhance vinegar to add more zest to your salads and cooked dishes. Herbs in season can be enjoyed all year long, once they have been introduced to vinegar and the process is simplicity itself.

It is possible to dump whatever herb you like right into the vinegar you choose and let the combination sit around until the flavors intermix. To be on the safe side, however, a bit of washing and boiling will help prevent strange things from cropping up in the finished elixir. Wash the fresh herb(s) you plan to use and dry thoroughly. Scald the bottles and let them dry out. Put the herbs in the bottles and cover them with vinegar that has been heated just to the boiling point. Let the bottles cool and then cap. Avoid using fresh sage, which works better when dried.

As a rule, the fresh herbs are left in the bottles, where they are not only attractive to the eye but make it easy to identify the flavor. Dried herbs should be strained off, in a day or two, after they have imparted their flavor, which they do more quickly than they do when fresh.

White wine vinegar is good for this, but in our house, we have gotten hooked on yellowish cider vinegar with tarragon. I also enjoy the more subtle Japanese rice vinegar. It may be the ultimate chic, but any old vinegar that isn't cloudy can be enhanced with judicious addition of other flavors. Flavored vinegars can be tiresome as a steady diet but they are fun to experiment with.

Dill and tarragon are basically so flavorful that they don't have to be tampered with before setting to steep. Milder herbs, like basil, will perform better if *slightly* crushed. Chives do well when cut in small strips. Let your imagination wander with you through your herb garden, if you are lucky enough to have one. Cloves of garlic and/or red and green peppers also make splendid and colorful vinegars. Most combinations will generate enough flavor to enjoy in a couple of weeks. Should they begin to get too strong, top up with more vinegar.

If you are wondering what to do with those exotic bottles hanging around that you can't bring yourself to throw away, make some flavored vinegars and jug them for Christmas or house-presents when you drop in for a drink or a week-end.

There's another good liquid to use in those extra bottles—vodka. I got the idea when I lunched at a Russian bistro in Paris. There, next to the pastry cart, was another rolling table loaded with liquid and herb-filled bottles. The herbs were the same but the liquid was vodka. The two I liked best were flavored with lemon and the hot, flaked red pepper. I have done some experimenting along the lines of the vinegar-flavoring method. The results were very tasty. I found that with carraway seeds, I could even make a passable Aquavit—not as good as the real thing, but o.k.

vinegar, a tenderizer?

Having spent several "no frills" years in Portugal and Spain, I ate my share of budget meals in simple places. More often than not, the cook operated only inches from the counter on which I ate some cheap but delicious meals. As a consequence, I learned a lot of tricks for converting economical raw materials into succulent dishes.

A favorite of mine has always been a *filete*, a very thin slice of some kind of meat, often snatched from a marinade in the ice box. The *filete* would be dropped onto a grill and as it cooked, rapidly, a splash of vinegar joined it as soon as it got warmed up. In the sherry areas of Spain, another splash of sherry was administered just before the final seconds of cooking.

I have turned many a piece of inexpensive meat into suppers that had 'em asking for more. I use a black iron skillet with a touch of olive oil to fry up my *filetes*. As soon as the meat is slightly browned, I add a spoonful of vinegar. (Putting it on at the beginning makes the meat stewy.) The sherry goes on at the end and I take the pan off the fire so that what hasn't vaporized can be poured over the *filetes* as sauce. I'm never sure just how much tenderizing effect the vinegar has, but—combined with the sherry—it gives a result that is certainly tasty. I suggest that you give it a whirl.

If you have slices of meat that are too thick for *filetes* and too thin to slice, you can flatten them with a meat pounder. I used to think that a gadget like this was a waste of money—until I bought one. It is a very handy tool to have and works much better than make-shift rolling-pins or bottles. A typical pounder is a flat, heavy metal disk with a handle. Gourmet shops sell them for under $10 and they are worth acquiring.

The sauce from doing the *filete* with vinegar and sherry is delicious but thin. It can be thickened into gravy with very little trouble for those who prefer a heartier topping. The same goes for roasting-pan drippings in general. Not to use them in some fashion is really a waste. Some people have no trouble turning out smooth gravies and sauces—others get lumpy results. This information can help you if you are in the second group.

roux & smooth sauces

To make a sauce or gravy from roasting pan juices or stock of some sort, you have to thicken it. There are various starches used to accomplish this— arrowroot, cornstarch, waxy maize, potato starch, rice flour, even breadcrumbs. Most commonly used, however, is regular flour.

Roux means a color between red and yellow in French, but a cooking roux goes from white to brown according to how long it is cooked. A light-colored roux thickens as much as three times more for its size than a dark one. To make a roux, you mix flour with butter—which gives the best taste, according to many people—and heat it long enough to transform the cereal flavor of the flour into something more tasty. (Chicken fat is also good, but, because of its more pronounced taste, its use depends on what it is going to thicken.) When the roux reaches a certain point—two or three minutes if you want it to stay white—it is added to the juice or stock, and together they gradually reach the consistency you desire. (Avoid aluminum saucepans— they can turn a roux grey.)

Many cookbooks explain making roux in great detail. Equal parts of flour and fat, combined before heating and stirred in vigorously to avoid lumps, etc. The method sounds ridiculously simple, but it can go wrong. It takes practice to judge when the flour and butter are mixed well enough to avoid lumping as well as the time it should be cooked to achieve a good taste of its own.

Good news!—there is an easy way to succeed at sauces and it's rarely mentioned in texts and hardly even advertised. Use a product named GOLD MEDAL WONDRA, an "instant" flour put out by General Mills in convenient-to-use 13.5 ounce shakers. It enables you to skip mixing the flour and butter at the start if you want. You can even skip the butter and just use it as a thickener, but the result won't taste as good.

You simply melt the butter and sprinkle the *Wondra* into it gently. Before you know it, you'll have a roux worthy of a master-chef. If you have a sauce already made but it isn't quite unctuous enough for you, you can dust the surface gingerly and stir while heating. You will still have to give it time to divest itself of the flour flavor but not as much as plain flour would require.

Note to *crêpe* lovers: This instant flour ranks right up there with the no-stick pan as hi-tech's gift to the French pancake maker. These very thin pancakes consist of flour, milk, eggs, butter and salt. When mixed, the traditional batter is supposed to rest for at least an hour for the flour to absorb the milk and make a smooth result. If you should wake up one morning with an insatiable desire for *crêpes*, instant flour in place of regular will allow you to have 'em on the table before your orange juice warms up.

Back in the sauce department: if you are not crazy about flour as a thickener for everything in spite of this remarkable instant flour, there's always cornstarch. It has a characteristic that flour does not share—that of rendering sauces more translucent than opaque. It also lends less of a taste of its own. I use it for thickening spaghetti sauce, which we make in large batches and freeze. When frozen sauce of this kind is thawed out, it gets a little watery and cornstarch does a fine, esthetically pleasing job of making it as good as new. I sometimes use cornstarch in place of flour when I am browning pieces of meat or chicken. It makes a crisper coating and doesn't cloud up the oil or butter as much as flour does.

7 | desserts and more

When it comes to desserts, I think we Americans have the edge on the rest of the world. Oh, there are a few pockets of luscious insanity such as Austria and Germany, where what they do with whipped cream does things to one's palate that borders on the obscene. With our over-processed dairy products, their desserts are tough for us to emulate. Pastry, which is quite good in England, is, to me, highly over-rated when the French make it. (Actually, the English call pastries "sweets" and reserve the term dessert for fruits and nuts —the ultimate course of a meal whose finale, "dessert", comes from the French *desservir* which means to clear the table.)

The Chinese, who have some of the greatest food in the world, apparently don't require anything more than lichee nuts and fortune cookies to kiss off their repasts, and we are probably just as well off as a result. If they came up with desserts to match their main dishes, we'd never be able to leave their tables to get hungry again an hour later. Iberians make such cloyingly sweet prandial post-scripts that they almost kill the pleasure of eating them. Italians, who are master cooks, wisely settle for fruit and cheese to end their meals.

So much for the rest of the world. I want to talk about our own desserts in the strictest sense. I mean things like pies, cakes and ice cream. Ice cream gets more popular and better and more expensive every year. French and Italian ices and ice creams are good, but they are living on their reputations, which are gradually fading in the light of our current competition. I haven't made ice cream for over forty years so I'm not going to dwell on the fine points of constructing it. In fact, I'm not even going to say much about eating same, preferring to use that time in consuming rather than expounding. I suspect that you might have similar feelings. The area that I live in has the highest per capita ice cream consumption nationwide—I'm not one to shirk my duty in upholding the statistics. But there is more to life than ice cream— *pie*, for example.

easy as pie

"As American as apple pie" is no accidental phrase. When it comes to pie, we've got it. At least, we had it. Good pie is not all that easy to find. My perennial pursuit of the perfect piece of pie has led me to the conclusion that home is where to find it. With the exception of some splendid crusty efforts I've found to be the rule, rather than the exception, in Pennsylvania Dutch country, real lip-smackers are rare indeed in commerce. I'm talkin' plain old pie here, not the gourmet extravaganzas that require a bank loan to purchase. I have nothing against them, especially when someone else is buying, but I do long for the simple piece of cherry pie, the kind that supposedly was found country-wide back in the good old days. If you share my predilection, hang on. Here's an easy way to make one yourself!

First of all, wash your hands! If you've got kids who want to help, have them do it too, twice. Despite the mystique of making pastry and the constant warnings about things that can go wrong, it is really very simple and it works best when you literally have a hand in it. Whichever way you decide to work, eschew those pastry-cutting knives and gadgets and let your fingers do the working. If you can't stand covering your hands in butter and flour, get some rubber gloves or, better still, a food processor.

You'll need flour, shortening, iced water and salt. Use plain old flour (all-purpose), not cake-flour which is too fine and sometimes has leavening built in. You'll note that this recipe calls for "2 cups of sifted flour." This means that you sift the flour *before* you measure it. Naturally, you shouldn't tamp it down in the measuring cup after it has been aerated. Just let the grains fall where they will into something that you know holds two cups. For shortening, I use a mixture of about ⅔ Crisco and ⅓ butter. You can vary these proportions to suit your pocketbook and taste.

Put the sifted flour and salt into a mixing bowl and begin to work the shortening through it gently with your fingers. After you have the ingredients fairly well distributed, start adding the water and work that around too. Don't dump the water in all at once. If it looks really moist, you can leave out the last tablespoon. Work the whole mess into a ball, sprinkle a little bit of flour on the outside so it won't be too sticky, and put the works in the refrigerator for at least ¾ of an hour, after which time you can assemble the pie of your dreams.

The point of this method is that it is simple and feasible by hand. There's no reason not to use a food processor if you prefer. Just dump in everything at once and whir for a very short time until it looks crumbly. Remove, roll into a ball and you're in business. Granted: the processor may mix faster, but somebody's got to wash it and that takes time too.

you can bake a cherry pie

Homemade cherry pie is high on my preferred list. (Rhubarb is really my favorite but relatives and friends have threatened to boycott this book if I feature it, so. . . .) If you are fortunate enough to have a cherry tree in your own yard, you're in luck. We did, way back when, but these days, most of us have to depend on canned cherries for our supply. If you buy the "just pour contents of can into a pie shell" variety, you'll be settling for less than the best. The already-prepared pie filling has sugar and other ingredients which you'll be shelling out a couple bucks a pound for. They are not only overpriced but also make a gluey, inferior pie to boot. So go for the cans of plain cherries and water. One regular can will be enough for a nine-inch pie.

And by the way—when recipes call for an 8- or a 9-inch pie pan, they usually don't bother to specify whether the measurement means the top or bottom of a sloped pie pan. To put my mind at ease on this score, I hunted around until I found a pan that was marked with its size on the bottom. Result: a nine-inch pie pan is nine inches across the top. While we're on pie pans—did you know that *Frisbees* are so called because the original frisbees were the pans left over from pies made by the *Frisbee Pie Company* in Connecticut—developed into sporting objects by playful pie-eating pupils!

You'll need the following: a #2 can of sour cherries, some sugar, salt, melted butter and tapioca. A tiny amount of almond extract enhances flavor, but many people do not like it. Mix all of these together and let them get acquainted while you roll out the pastry.

Perhaps you are wondering what tapioca is doing in there with the cherries. If you had only cherries, sugar and water, the combination would stay quite fluid and sink into the crust. To thicken liquid mixtures in general, cooks have a choice of flour, cornstarch or tapioca. Flour retains some taste when cooked and turns a pie filling somewhat opaque—not particularly appetizing to look at or eat. Cornstarch is relatively tasteless and effects a translucent result as a thickener. However, it has to be stirred around whatever you're using it in to keep it from clumping, an inefficient process when dealing with fragile cherries.

Tapioca is easily dispersed with a few deft turns of the spoon. It affords an esthetically pleasing consistency and a nearly neutral flavor. Ergo, use tapioca, not *Argo* (brand name of a popular cornstarch). I'm not talking about tapioca the size of BB shot that you may have had in your high-chair or in elementary school, where they were generally known as fish-eyes. Use the granulated variety. It goes well with rhubarb too!

As a final tapioca note: in case someone works it into a Trivial Pursuit question, tapioca comes from the manioc root, a staple root-vegetable grown in the tropics. The manioc is shaved into water, swirled, and spattered onto a hot surface where it makes itself into pellets. And now to create *the* pie.

Divide the chilled dough into two hunks, one a little bit larger than the other. Sprinkle flour on the board, table or marble slab you have chosen for rolling, some on your rolling pin and maybe a little on your hands so that you can work these two hunks into spheres. Roll out the larger one first. Go up and down, then side to side so as to work the piece of pastry into a circle a little larger than the top of your pie pan. It may take a couple of tries at first but it won't take long to get the hang of rolling dough. If your piece of dough looks too square, start over. If it starts to stick to the pin or the board, dust on a *little bit* more flour. Beware of over-flouring. Settle for a sloppy looking pie rather than crumby pastry.

Once your circle is big enough, transfer it to the pan. It may make it easier to move if you fold it over on itself to transport. When you really get into baking, you'll probably get used to picking up the dough on the roller (making sure it has enough flour on it so the circle won't stick to the pin). If you've never done this before, it's a good idea to watch someone else demonstrate. If you have no baking friends, you can always be on the look-out for a Julia Child re-run. She makes rolling dough look easy for the simple reason that—with a little practice—it is! Many people fail in pastry-making and life in general because they try too hard. Moderation has a way of paying off, in this case, with nice, flaky tasty pie crust.

With the bottom crust in the pan, roll out the top and get it ready. After you pour in the cherries, lay on the cover and use the tines of a fork to crimp its edge, fastening it to the pastry already in place. Cut a few holes in the top crust to let the steam escape once the filling heats up. This will help to avoid volcanoes from forming in your oven, gurgling cherry-lava over everything.

As soon as you think the oven has arrived at 450 degrees, pop in the pie and note the time. This initial high heat helps set the pastry before the juices can infiltrate and sog it up. When 10 minutes are up, reduce the heat to 350 degrees and bake for another 25 minutes or so. You'll have a dessert fit for G. Washington himself!

vinegar pie and crust

Some people have a lot of trouble making pastry. I was discussing this with a Yankee doctor friend of mine who passed this recipe on to me. A friend of his was ready to give up pies forever, until she discovered the vinegar method. She swears it's the vinegar that gives her the crust to keep rolling. I found it worked quite well with very little struggle. The pastry has a slightly different taste and texture. I think it's better with fillings like creamed chicken or meat and I prefer the first recipe for fruit pies.

In one bowl, mix flour, shortening, water and sugar. In another, mix an egg, salt and vinegar. Knead the two together and refrigerate for half an hour. From there on, continue in the usual way.

I looked for this vinegar crust in quite a few cookbooks. The only vinegar-related pies I found were two using vinegar for the filling. Both of them came out fine and were quickly gobbled up. These hundred-year-old Virginia recipes are in the back if you want to experiment. The recipes, as I found them, made a dull-looking filling, so I added some green coloring drops and had guests guess what they were sampling.

words about ovens

Most cooks prefer gas ovens. So do I. Unfortunately, our house is not near a city gas line and we've never gotten up the nerve to have a propane tank decorating the side of the house. After a lot of research, I decided to give a table Turbo-convection model a whirl to take some of the load off of our big, not-very-efficient wall model. Our turbo is made by Farberware, cost under $200 and sits on the counter, where it works like a charm. It's a class item. For example, they've used real chrome on the bottom pan so that anything that drips on it is not instantly welded to the surface for keeps.

In theory, a turbo oven performs the same jobs as conventional ovens at lower temperatures and in less time per project. In this respect, I suspect that the manufacturer is indulging in a bit of hyperbole. Of course it could be that our electricity is not as potent as that in the Farberware testing laboratory.

Whatever the case may be, I have found that I can reduce either time or temperature but not both to the "suggested" amounts at the same time. The rest of the oven instructions have proved to be impeccable. I was particularly interested to learn from them that a glass pie pan will not give as good a crust as a metal one, at least in their oven. All in all, it's one of the best purchases I've made in a long time, much better than a new asparagus steamer, which is two inches shorter than asparagus seems to grow.

easier than pie

There's an overseas relative of pie that is much easier to make and somewhat richer. It's English nanny-food, known around countless nurseries as apple crumble. Not only is it simplicity itself to create, but, for my money, also beats the crust off apple pie as a desirable dessert. American cookbooks show nothing between crullers and crumpets, perhaps because crumbles are too uncomplicated. Like trifles, another English favorite (theirs not mine), crumbles are thrown together with what's in the larder.

You'll need some fruit, flour, dark brown sugar, regular sugar, lots of butter, some lemon juice and cinnamon. Apples make a great crumble so let's use them for our fruit. Dice about a pound of them, leaving the peels on. Preparation is short, so turn the oven on to heat at 300 degrees. Combine the brown sugar and flour and mix in the butter (in chunks) with your fingers. Work the butter in until it forms crumbles, particles that look like king-sized breadcrumbs. Put the apples in a deep pie dish, add lemon juice and sprinkle on white sugar and cinnamon. Put the crumbles on top of the apples and company, covering the whole surface. Tamp down ever so lightly and bake for 15 minutes.

When the topping has turned crusty and you can see bubbles here and there, the crumble is done. If this doesn't happen in a quarter of an hour, leave it in another 5 or more minutes. If you haven't over-tamped the crumble, some of the crusty lumps may fall down into the middle—a very desirable result that I try to arrange in advance. The English sometimes serve it with thick cream or custard. I like it straight, hot or cold.

Other fruits also make fine crumbles, particularly rhubarb. The latter is sour, compared to apples, so you will want to add more sugar and less lemon juice if you use it. Children love making crumbles almost as much as eating them. Let 'em take a shot at it when you feel adventurous and lazy at the same time.

meringues

In Section 6, when we got into homemade mayo, I promised you a way to use up those leftover egg whites. The two main choices in our household are angel food cakes and meringues. I'm going to leave the former for the next book. Unless you've had a lot of experience around the kitchen, you'll have a devil of a time making angel food, whereas meringues are even easier than crumbles. These light, white pastries are delectable taken straight. For fancier treats, they make good vehicles for ice cream and chocolate sauce or whipped cream. You won't have any trouble getting rid of meringues unless you are surrounded by low-sugar dieters.

A basic meringue is made of egg whites and sugar. (The finer the sugar, the better, but ordinary granulated *will* work.) If you've made the 6-egg mayonnaise, 1½ cups of sugar will handle the leftover 6 whites conveniently. You whip the whites in an ultra-clean bowl until they form soft peaks. The slightest speck of leftover mayo or any other oil-bearing residue will prevent the egg whites from performing at peak perfection. When the beaten egg whites form little hills in the bowl, leave the mixer on and gradually add the sugar until the mixture gets stiff. Don't be afraid to flagellate the whites—as long as 5 or 10 minutes would not be excessive but hardly necessary. Ladle out tablespoonfuls on a cookie sheet, leaving a good inch between globs. If you don't have non-stick utensils, you should put a piece of brown paper on the pan before you deposit the little clouds—cleaning up will be easier.

For the final step, use a barely warm oven. Meringues work best when "dried out" rather than subjected to a lot of heat. If your schedule allows it, the best system is to shove them in the oven after you've finished something in it at regular roasting temperature. Turn the oven off and let it cool down a bit. Leave the meringues in as long as you can—overnight is good. In any event, keep the temperature below *200* degrees, should you feel the urge to turn the oven back on.

These no-frills meringues may be too bland for your taste when eaten just plain. They will, however, make a great base for fancy desserts. A glance at most meringue recipes will show various proportions and additional ingredients leading to more savory results. Also, some cooks recommend adding cream of tartar while whipping. Cream of tartar is not for taste but to help keep the egg whites fluffy but firm. Salt may be called for but it is not necessary. A splash of vanilla and/or almond extract won't hurt if you like a little more flavor. There's no harm in trying out any or all of these additions to achieve the meringue of your dreams.

Even if the meringues don't turn out picture-book perfect, they'll still be good. If they get a little dark as a result of too much heat, they are still delicious. If they get very dry, they'll be just that much better with ice cream and/or fruit. And when they get those little beads of gold on the outside from fighting off humidity, they're simply chewy to eat but very worth while. The kicker is that they are very impressive. Guests who drop in will be astonished when you offer them some *meringues glacées,* i.e., meringues with ice cream or sherbert and possibly some sauce on top. If they haven't read this book, they'll probably never know how easy it was to make such a treat.

Just a couple of things—if they are not all gobbled up right after you make them, store meringues in an air-tight container at room temperature. Try to use them up soon so that you can make more. Also, wait for a dry day the first time you make meringues. The lower the humidity, the better they work.

macaroons

It's a moot point at which stage a meringue becomes a macaroon. One basic difference is density. Meringues are light; macaroons are not. Classic macaroon recipes call for sugar syrup and lots of bother, but very acceptable ones can be made by embellishing the basic meringue formula.

A portion of coconut added to the meringue mix will change its consistency considerably. Such a thicker mixture needs a hotter oven—around 300 degrees—and shouldn't take longer than a half-hour to turn into mouth-ready macaroons.

Almond macaroons can take even less effort. Pulverize a half pound of plain almonds in your blender and mix them into 3 egg whites a little at a time. You don't even have to whip the whites. Add a pound of sugar and mix well. Place flattened little spoonfuls on a cookie sheet and bake them the same as the coconut macaroons.

The first time I tried the almond bits, I was a little casual about measuring the egg whites. The leftover ones had been frozen and they had to be thawed out. As a rule, once they become liquid again, it's easy to judge "one" egg, because a whole white makes a distinct plop when poured out. This time, some extra-runny part got into the act and threw things out of proportion. My would-be macaroons spread over the cookie sheet like a pool of mercury. I wasn't up to starting over so I baked the lake. It was a new kind of candy but —better still—crumbled, it made a perfect topping for a dish of vanilla ice cream. The next time I made macaroons, I made some more the accidental way, as well as regulars, for which I whipped the whites.

the daily apples—southern fried

The dish that follows is so vital to me that I wanted to start off the book with it. My gourmet consultants allowed as how not everyone would find it as delectable as I do. A compromise has been made. Even though it's breakfast food to me, it's good enough to qualify for lunch, dinner and in between, so it's going to keep company with the desserts. Try it any old time, whatever you decide it is.

There are few things more pleasant to wake up to than the aroma of sizzling bacon working its way across the pillow. Among the many nostalgic scenes of yesteryear that self-conjure at bacon's call are the halcyon days spent visiting my Uncle Jimmy and Aunt Lillian in Lynchburg, Virginia.

Bacon at Uncle Jimmy's held more than its usual promise elsewhere because it was invariably the harbinger of my favorite breakfast food, fried apples.

For a good seventy of his more than four score years, Uncle Jimmy had fried apples approximately 358 mornings a year. He was an early riser—an avuncular trait passed down to me—and he was always the first to rattle the kitchen hardware in the wee hours of dawn. He used to whistle C. & W. from the very start of operations. I loved it, but the tunes drove Aunt Lil' up the wall. She wasn't a real fried-apple freak, either, but her conclusion was that she could suffer through the traditional early morning concert and menu with minimal reluctance when the alternative was jumping out of bed to join the first shift at breakfast. A properly fried apple takes a fair amount of time— up to an hour—and Lil' was quite content to linger alone while the rest of us took on our ritual fix.

You will rarely find fried apples in cookbooks. The recipes I *have* found are *not* what I call the real thing. I've seen recipes with egg and cinnamon— forget them. To produce the finest, you'll need apples, bacon, brown sugar and a frying pan, preferably a big, old, heavy, black one made of cast iron.

Cook up 4 or 5 rashers of bacon per person. Don't hurry it. The more slowly bacon cooks, the better it will be. Besides, you'll need some time to slice up your apples. Any apples will do, but I prefer firm ones with a little zing in their taste—the kind that, in the words of Aunt Lil', "make your jaws ring." Granny Smiths are perfect and they are getting easier to find every day. Allow 2 or 3 apples per person and cut them in ½- to ¾-inch wedges. Leave the skins on. Sprinkle a little brown sugar over the pieces of apple and mix them around enough to get coated with it.

By this time, the bacon should be done. Take it out of the pan and dump the apples into the nice pool of bacon drippings. The way a lot of bacon arrives these days, you'll be lucky to have much lean anyway, but never mind, the fat is what makes good apples even better. I realize that there's a lot of negative propaganda about bacon—fat or lean—but some sacrifices to longevity just have to be made to enable us to enjoy the shorter years. Who knows? If Uncle Jimmy had cut down to, say, three times a week, he might still be with us, wondering what to eat those other four mornings. He figured that life is not a dress rehearsal. Since we only go around once, make the best of each day. For him and me, fried apples are right up there with the rest of the best.

If you are worried about shortening your life by taking on all those drippings, pour some off. You don't have to waste them. We mix our surplus bacon fat with cornmeal and make blocks of birdfood out of it. Birds really dig the combination.

At any rate, get the apples frying and as they begin to soften, mash them down a bit. Add just a little water if they get too dry. The amounts of sugar and water you need to use will depend strictly on the quality of the apples. Only experience will help you get the measurements under control. As in trying anything new, use less water and/or sugar rather than more. You aren't trying for applesauce. When they reach a consistency you like, serve up the fried apples with buttered toast, hot coffee, and all that nice crisp bacon. I don't know how to write "ummm-ummph" and make it sound Southern, but you'll be sure to say something like it the first time you try them. How about "ummm-ummph, y'all?"

Fried apples will keep several days in the refrigerator. If you happen on a choice basket of windfalls, let yourself go and fry up a big batch. This way, there will be a change-of-pace breakfast available whenever you feel like one. Don't worry, they won't stick around long once the word gets out about how good they are.

micro-fried granny smiths?

As fond as I am of traditional fried apples, I usually have other chores in the morning that make it tough to stand over the skillet the length of time it requires to do them Uncle Jimmy's way. As a result, I have experimented with the microwave oven and come up with an acceptable substitute. I'm not sure whether "acceptable" is the way some of the rest of my family would describe the dish, but I haven't had any rejects yet. Here's a hi-tech approach to try. It's practical only for small quantities. Microwave cooking time depends on the volume of what's cooked, so you wouldn't save any time feeding more than one or two people.

Cut the bacon in one-inch pieces and shove them in the micro in a non-metallic deep dish. While they are crisping up, cut the apples. By the time you've dusted them with the brown sugar, the bacon will be done. Add the apples, leaving the bacon and drippings in the dish. Pour in a couple of shooters of white wine (or water) and cook on high for 3 or 4 minutes.

Then mash down the apples and put the heat back on, this time on medium or low. Set the oven for about 7 minutes and turn on the "browner" element if you have one. (The browner element will make an almost gummy top layer which is very palatable. Stop and stir once or twice to distribute this taste-touch topping throughout the mash.) They are going to be great, but they are also going to be hotter than Tophet or Chinese take-out! I came close to terminal palate burn-out in my haste to sample a batch not long ago. They weren't worth it. Let the apple heat taper off before you take an indiscriminate bite.

Note: You can settle for the best of both worlds by combining the two methods. Use the micro to soften up the apples and *then* dump them in the frying pan containing the drippings from bacon cooked the old-fashioned way.

pancakes you'll really flip over!

As long as we're below the Mason-Dixon line, I want to bring up another Southern specialty. Anyone involved in the eternal search for something "different" for breakfast is hereby advised to check out corn cakes. These are really just pancakes made with cornmeal instead of flour. They have probably escaped universal notice because they require a step or two more to prepare than regular pancakes. The latter, for many, involves only opening a box of mix or a trip to a fast-food joint. Once you've tried corn cakes, you just may have a change of heart and eat a real breakfast.

The most difficult part of making corn cakes is finding the "right" cornmeal. Roughly, there are two categories: old-fashioned and mass-produced. Mass-produced is what you find in the cereal and flour section of the supermarket. It has been milled like flour, somewhat refined and degerminated so that it will have a long shelf life. Alas, the taste of the germ is what separates the "right" cornmeal from all the rest. The old-fashioned kind is ground between millstones. These operate at a lower temperature, which keeps taste-changing to a minimum, and allows the germ and the bran to stay in so that you can experience a more pronounced taste in whatever you use it for. This rougher cornmeal also accounts for the lacy texture of real corn cakes.

My mother has been on a long look-out for two things: "The Fountain of Youth" and "water-ground" cornmeal. I think she's found the former, but a request for the latter draws a blank from all but old-timers who remember water-powered mills as part of the landscape. You can get stone-ground cornmeal in health food stores along with a lecture on how much better it is for you than the other kind. So buy stone-ground. While you can make corn cakes with the regular type, it's worth the trip (and the lecture) to visit one of those places where *everything* is natural.

Mix the dry ingredients—cornmeal, salt, sugar and baking powder—and beat in egg, melted butter and milk. Drop spoonfuls on a greased medium-hot griddle and watch the big bubbles come to the surface. Don't pour the batter onto the griddle—use a spoon. The cornmeal sinks to the bottom of the batter no matter how often you stir it, so pouring gets mostly milk with the basic batter. Flip once, cook until done and serve with butter and syrup. This is a thin batter and the cakes will look like golden lace. They are fragile and delicious. You'll wait a long time before flipping over those other cottony ordinary pancakes again.

Note: The above is the way you *might* find the recipe in an old-fashioned cook book. Unfortunately, an important instruction is left out, because a good many cooking books were (and still are) written for people who already knew how to cook. You're in trouble if you don't realize that, for some recipes, cornmeal should be allowed to soak up liquid before cooking with it. This is a case in point. Unless you pre-soak the meal a few minutes, you'll have a difficult time maneuvering these delicate cakes around the griddle. You risk having a soggy lump in the middle of each dropping, with the milk running around every which way. So, warm the milk first and then slosh the cornmeal and salt and sugar through it until it's a relatively homogeneous mixture. Put in the baking powder *last* of all, just before making the cakes. Very hot milk can cause the baking powder to fritter away its gas before its time.

The Commonwealth Club of Richmond, Virginia, raised corn cakes to epicurean heights by combining them with broiled oysters and ham — Smithfield, of course. Thin slices of ham were lightly broiled and placed on top of a stack of six 4-inch wide corn cakes. Oysters, pan-broiled with butter, Worcestershire sauce and celery salt, then went on top of the ham. A *cloche* (glass bell), capped each plate, which was then whisked to the table to be eaten at once.

spoonbread

In the South these days, you are liable to run into spoonbread, which is another delicious way to use cornmeal. Spoonbread tastes a little like cornbread but has a texture more like a solid soufflé. It is spooned out of a bowl as a side dish to a variety of main courses. A genuine, traditional spoonbread calls for buttermilk, but like water-ground cornmeal, real buttermilk is not easy to find if you don't live on a farm. What masquerades as buttermilk these days is more like liquid yoghurt, and — while some of it tastes good — its chemical make-up keeps it from working properly in old-fashioned recipes. That being the case, here's a very simple method to turn out an acceptable spoonbread without it.

In place of buttermilk, which reacts with baking soda to provide leavening, you use sweet milk and baking powder. Cornmeal is put into boiling water to swell up. Then butter and salt are added to it, plus cool milk to lower the temperature. You are going to add eggs and baking powder that you don't want to start cooking before everything goes into a very hot oven. Bake it in a bowl you can take to the table. Try to time things so that it is ready when supper is—it is at its best piping hot.

Spoonbread does wonders for a country meal. 'Tain't bad in the city either!

pão-de-ló (portuguese café cake)

I used to eat *Pão-de-Ló* every day in *Sines*. *Sines* (pronounced See-nesh) is a fishing town down the coast from Lisbon. It is known for being the birthplace of *Vasco da Gama* and the location of the biggest, ugliest oil refinery ever to ruin a once fantastically beautiful seaside village. The pure, pre-refinery salt air was quite an appetite stimulator and the Portuguese were and are always ready for some sort of *bolo* (cake) and coffee to stave off hunger pains.

Daily, about 3 p.m., my favorite *Sines* café produced hot pans of *Pão-de-Ló*, a type of sponge cake that other cuisines generally make with only eggs, sugar and flour. *Pão* is Portuguese for bread and *Ló* is from loaf in English, but this is far from a loaf of bread. The Sines version goes a couple of steps beyond ordinary sponge cake by adding olive oil and honey to the ingredients! Even though Portuguese oil and honey are much more highly flavored than we are accustomed to, somehow, both of these rather strong flavors seem to calm each other down to a mild and mellow marriage. Here's how you can taste some on this side of the ocean. You will be astonished to find that the olive taste is there only to those who know what went into the cake.

To make some *Pão-de-Ló*, bring a cup of honey and a cup of olive oil to a boil together. While the mixture is cooling down, beat a cup of sugar into 7 egg yokes and combine it with the honey and oil when tepid. Sift a teaspoon of baking powder with 2 to 3 cups of flour (amount depending on consistency of honey you use) and incorporate this into the yoke mixture. The 7 egg whites are to be whipped well and folded gently into the batter, which is in turn poured into a greased pan. Sure, use a little more olive oil for this—might as well go whole hog. Sprinkle in a little grated nutmeg for authenticity. Bake for about three-quarters of an hour at 330 degrees. You'll be the first on the block with a *Sines Pão-de-Ló*.

8 | in remembrance of meals past

Why should meals take a permanent place in my memory? I can't answer that, but I know that they do. The events and places I am describing to you come directly from somewhere inside my head, not a note-book. I have found that keeping notes gives me license to forget. What I don't remember wasn't worth remembering, I rationalize.

As I relive these experiences, I can see the places where they happened. This is easy for me because I am, first of all, a painter. When I look at paintings from years ago, I sometimes remember what I was hearing at the time —the sounds around me or music and stories from some sort of ever-present internal radio. Along with the other memories that come filtering through from paintings are the smells and tastes of the surroundings and the food and drink I experienced in them. In the hope that you will enjoy sharing such personal memories with me, I offer a few "unforgettable" incidents. Perhaps they will evoke your own souvenirs and help you enjoy re-membering all those times you may have thought had faded away forever.

The first time I did some room-service ordering in Paris, I ordered some sliced chicken and wine only to receive a ham sandwich and a bottle of beer. From then on, I adopted the habit of speaking English first until my French surpassed the English of waiters and sales personnel that I encountered. As a student in France, I was eager to soak up as much of the French spirit as I could. Facility in French finally allowed me to become more daring in choosing my meals than asking for chicken and ham.

The next trip to Paris *en famille* was something else. By then I was ready to tackle almost anything reputedly edible that didn't bite first and, what's more, able to ask for it in its native tongue.

In return for the hospitality he had enjoyed thanks to our southern relatives, a French magnate invited my mother and me to partake of some of the luxurious aspects of Paris. At the time, his company was negotiating for some stateside holdings of our family and we were the only ones of our relatives inclined to visit Europe. We were to be wined and dined — an expression that reaches its epitome in "the City of Light."

Our first night on the town started with a splendid dinner at the *Tour d'Argent*, a lovely restaurant facing Notre Dame that lived up to its worldwide reputation. Our host was not the top man of the firm but an executive in charge of feting visiting firemen. He was as charmed with us as we were with him and he invited us out the next day. He took us to the Jockey Club for a drink — after which we picked up his mistress and headed for dinner. The restaurant he chose for us was *Chez Françoise*, highly recommended by the Michelin Guide and located, of all places, in a bus station. This particular bus station is *l'Aérogare d'Orly*, where one boards buses for the airport. The opulence may have been a few degrees below that of the *Tour d'Argent* but our host pointed out that we were his personal guests — in other words, not on the company expense account. In any event, *Chez Françoise* is also where I had one of the best meals I can remember ever eating — anywhere.

It started with three different small pastries, tarts garnished with peppery Basque concoctions of sausage, onions and tomato-pimento. For me, our host had suggested *Rable de Lièvre Châtelaine*, saddle of hare. Soon after the tasty tarts were history, I was presented with succulent slices of juicy hare, enveloped with velvety, dark brown sauce and accompanied by purées of chestnut and potatoes with celery. The main course was so good that I can just barely remember the *profiteroles* I had for dessert. This meal banished me forever from the "eat to live" camp and stamped my psyche "epicure" until my liver gives out.

It hasn't been all downhill since, thank goodness, but that meal was definitely it for our Paris trip that year. The following day, the head of the firm, undoubtedly regaled with tales of our mutual pleasure by his assistant,

HARE

escorted us to Maxim's. There, I had stuffed veal for the first and last time. The most intriguing aspects of our meal at Maxim's were the delightful costume of the after-dinner coffee server and the way the staff literally lined up at the door to have their palms crossed as we left. It was indeed exciting and interesting to be the honored guests of a millionaire industrialist.

The next time I returned to Paris, I made a bee-line for *Chez Françoise*. *Rable de Lièvre* was on the menu and I ordered it. As I was mopping up the last puddle of sauce, the waiter asked how I had enjoyed my meal. I in turn asked if I could start it over again and I did. I'm looking forward to the day(s) when I can do it again, and again. . . .

Hares are somewhat scarce where I live now so I haven't had occasion to cook one recently. However, the recipe is one that will make it easier to imagine how good it would taste and can be used for other meats. It makes a very fine pseudo-Sauerbraten:

Start by studding the saddle with a few strips of salt pork and put it in a crock with an approximation of the following: a cup of red wine, a cup of vinegar, 2 cups of water, a sliced onion, a sliced carrot, a clove or two of garlic, herbs of your choice and salt and pepper. Turn this over a few times during the next four days and let the marinade do its job.

An hour or so before your meal, take the saddle out, dry it, roast it in a HOT oven for around 20 minutes. (A heavier piece of meat will require more time roasting.) Take the saddle out of the roasting pan and keep it warm. Add to the roasting pan a cup of brandy (all right, *half* a cup), a third of a cup of the marinade and reduce over high heat for a few minutes. When it thickens up, add a cup of cream and cook for another 3 minutes. Slice the meat and pour the sauce over it. It's hard to imagine any meat that wouldn't be good prepared this way.

By the way—don't throw the rest of the marinade away—it will make a good base for soup or sauce for something else.

Though the following took place before the Paris hare, it's equally memorable. I put it in second place because one of the specialties we had might not be enjoyed by all. I include it because it's the sort of thing one should be prepared for in a different culture, not because I want you to rush out with a BB gun and try for more of the same.

But first, a little atmosphere . . . Roquefort-sur-Soulzon is a hamlet deep down in the Southern part of France where they've been making cheese for centuries. There, they use ewes' milk for their product and call it *Roquefort*. Other countries make similar cheeses, which we lump together under the heading of "blue cheese" (except Stilton and Gorgonzola, which merit their own handles), but there is only one genuine *Roquefort* and this is where it comes from.

There, ewes' milk is turned to curds which, when formed into roughly three-pound wheels, are stashed in cool caves to ripen. They soon develop

Penicillium roqueforti, the green mold that give blue cheese its distinctive appearance and flavor. To get the mold to spread through the cheese, the *petits vieux fromagers* (little ol' cheesemakers) run them through with a needle-bearing device not unlike the gadget used to hold flowers in an arrangement.

The hills around Roquefort are riddled with shored-up caverns where the cheeses sojourn until ready for market. No matter how carefully they are handled, the cheeses mature at their own speeds and to their own consistencies. As they mature, they are sorted out for different markets around the world. The ones that start to crawl off the tables get sent to Marseilles, where heavy tastes are popular. The more stolidly bland specimens are scheduled for the U. S. of A. You can see the little signs marking destinations if you are lucky enough to visit the caves — highly recommended on a hot day — especially if you like cheese.

After a trip through the cheese vaults, a visit to the *Grand Hotel* is a must. If there is a way to improve anything with Roquefort, they've figured it out at this modest hotel cum restaurant. Not to worry — they don't put it in *everything*. But what they do use it in is great, to me, and I'm not even a Roquefort fanatic. In fact, among several memorable meals there, this one engraved itself on my unforgettable list for ingredients not even kin to cheese.

I was dining there with my mother who is, to say the least, difficult to please when it comes to food unless either she prepares it or it's made of chocolate. At any rate, we were seated most cordially and within minutes, out came the chef with a grin almost as important as his tall white hat. He was carrying a small tray bearing something obviously very precious. He zeroed in on Mother, uncovered his treasure and offered, *"Voilà Madame, une specialité d'aujourd'hui!"* He removed a napkin to display a nest containing half a dozen fuzzy, limp little birds, larks as I recall — ones that had taken their last flights.

The sight of the tiny cadavers gave Mother quite a start. I must confess that I was also shaken, it being my first year abroad during which I was still learning that some facts of life there are different. I tried to soft pedal Mom's near-shriek with some elementary French meant to discourage further exposure to the situation. I was sure that the chef understood after he did a fast 180 back to his stoves, leaving the way open for the headwaiter to come back for our formal order.

We pretty much got our desires across by some judicious pointing and pigeon-French. At least we thought we did. Back in those 1950s, about five Americans a year came through Roquefort-sur-Soulzon and the other three probably would have spoken French.

We savored our way through *Feuilletés à la façon de Roquefort* (puff pastry with you-know-what tastefully worked through it). I had some crawfish with cream and we were both waiting for the next course, chicken with morels, when back out came the chef with his treasure, transformed. He had mistaken my Mother's excitement for ecstasy and put the finishing touches to the larks. This time they were defeathered, roasted to a turn and reposing in a delicate nest of golden shoestring potatoes, their little beaks fully open as they might have been in a final plea for mercy. The moment was definitely critical.

This time, Mother convinced the chef that she had all she could handle with the hors-d'oeuvres and the chicken. He smiled and left us to finish our dinner sans birds. My room-service "chicken and ham" French decidedly needed some refinement.

That was the end of the larks as far as we were concerned. But, the next morning, as we were putting on our MG TD to head south, we heard, *"Attendez Monsieur-Dame, nous avons quelque chose pour vous!"* The happy chef came pattering across the courtyard to unroll Act III of his *specialité.* With infinite charm, he presented Mother with a small cardboard box containing the birds in their nest to enjoy on the road. The contents *were* enjoyed but not by either of us. I took them home to our hosts in Montpellier, where they were gleefully crunched by Monsieur, heads and all.

I must confess that I eventually overcame my better instincts and gingerly joined the bird-eating crowd. Almost everywhere in Europe they are considered a delicacy, with reason. They are, in a word, delicious. They are served in restaurants and cafés, not to mention bars and roadside stands. One of my favorite sidewalk signs in Spain *"Hoy, no hay"*—which means "Today, we don't have any"—almost always refers to birds!

Students of French may recall the gay little song that goes: *"Alouette, gentille alouette . . . Je te plumerai la tête . . . etc."* This translates roughly as:

"Lark, nice lark . . . I shall pluck the feathers from your head . . . etc." The French have undoubtedly been singing some version of this for nearly as long as they've been eating larks, which, incidentally, are at their best in autumn. Should you ever wish to try out your appetite for small birds—you know, if one runs into your windshield or something—here's how to prepare them:

Unlike larger game birds, they are neither hung nor cleaned except for the gizzard, which may contain unpalatable pebbles and bird junk-food. Pull out their feathers, flame them to remove the feather ends you may have missed, wrap them with a strip or two of bacon and drop in a frying pan with butter for about 10 minutes over a hot fire. Serve on toast with wedges of lemon. Be sure not to invite any Audubon Society members to share your goodies.

the first and last? tamale

Even though what follows was long after and far away, I wonder how the Roquefort chef would have reacted to my first memorable Mexican *merienda*. (That's Spanish for an afternoon snack.) Alas, I was dining alone, at a roadside café near Veracruz. Up until then, I had been eating mostly in my camper, a bit leery of experiencing local fare after the many warnings I had heard about the things that happen to casual eaters south of the border. I was tired of "playing it safe" so I pulled over to indulge in local color.

Not much was stirring when I arrived. Somewhere back under the banyan trees a guitar was softly adding atmosphere. All able bodies in sight were prone. Far be it from me to break up anyone's siesta with a shout, so I sat down and lighted my pipe. I felt that my presence was sensed, but the "observers" were probably hoping I'd just go away. I was happy to be part of the scenery. I sure hadn't stumbled into a fast-food outlet.

Eventually, a small boy in a large sombrero went over to shake the chef out of his hammock, pointing at the waiting stranger. They decided that I was there to stay, so together they came to see what they could do for me. I asked for a beer and something to eat.

While the boy went off to fetch my beer, the chef plucked what looked *something* like a flattened ear of corn from a laundry tub of bubbling water, conveniently located about five feet from where I was sitting. "Would the Señor like a nice hot tamale, made this morning?" For the benefit of those who have yet to sample one of these and have little desire to risk one, a tamale is a zippy concoction of cornmeal and/or meat and spices—pretty much anything that can be ground up and tastes good. Everything is tightly wrapped in banana leaves or corn husks and put to steep in a steamy container of water. They always say not to eat anything you can't peel or boil in Mexico. This looked almost safe on both counts, so I went for it.

The first bite was sheer pleasure. What had I been missing? As I neared the end of the tamale, a scraggly old setter ambled by to survey the scene.

Seeing that I wasn't prepared to share my *merienda* with him, he shuffled off into the dust, pausing at the tamale cauldron to lift his leg and add a new nuance to the brew.

I settled for one tamale that afternoon. As a matter of fact, neither that tamale nor anything else I ate in Mexico ever came near to upsetting my breadbasket. It wasn't until I was on my way back home, when — deep in the heart of Texas — I was done in by a chili-dog I had the temerity to order in a seemingly sterile beanery.

le pique-nique

Contrary to popular belief, the French are extremely sociable, once certain hurdles are surmounted. The language barrier is the principal impediment to getting friendly with the French, but it can be more than adequately compensated for by an expressed interest in pleasures of the table. It is rare for any but the most intimate of friends to be invited to a French home — foreigners stand even slimmer chances, even when meeting a French family might involve a business deal of some import. In such a case, you might be invited to dine out in a restaurant. But there is a half-way meeting ground on which *un étranger* could conceivably make the grade — by participating in *un pique-nique*. If you ever stumble into such an occasion, grab the chance. A French picnic is something else.

We have borrowed the word "picnic" from our French allies. For them, the word is made up of two verbs: *piquer* and *niquer*. The first comes from

le pique-nique .

old French and means "little thing," at least as it is involved with *pique-nique*. *Niquer* originally meant a shake of the head, usually in mistrust or mockery of someone. (It is more currently employed as a rather vulgar expression for fornication, which can sometimes occur after a smashing *pique-nique*, but that's for some other tale to come.) The combination has evolved into a meal taken *en plein air, sur l'herbe*, as in *déjeuner sur l'herbe*, from the famous painting of the same name.

My first *pique-nique* took place when I was living with the family in Southern France where I was tutoring and picking grapes. As practically a member of the family, I was invited along for Sunday outings. My previous picnics had been along the lines of fried chicken, pickles, potato salad and punch. I was quite unprepared for what was to be put before me once we got out into the French countryside. Getting there was a new adventure, too.

My hosts had just acquired a *Deux Chevaux* (two horsepower), *Citroen's* answer to the Volkswagen. At the time (1951), feeling was still running high against the Germans and most Frenchmen would rather have been shot than caught circulating in a German automobile.

For those who may never have experienced a *Deux Chevaux*, it is rather like riding in a half-squeezed accordion, which it resembles because of its corrugated metal sides. In truth, there has probably never been any other car as practical to own and maintain. What it lacked in comfort, it made up for in versatility and reliability. It had front-wheel drive, so it could go just about anywhere and, most important for picnics, the very comfortable seats could be plucked from the chassis and used *ex-machina* anywhere a carefree crowd decided to pull up. With three adults and four children (*and* enough food for a regiment), we didn't exactly burn up the highway, but we had a lot of fun navigating the few kilometres into the nearby mountains.

Of the many outings I was lucky enough to share, I particularly remember one of the very first ones at the site of *Saint Guilhem le Desert. St. Guilhem* is a tiny village nestled in a time warp about 25 kilometres from Montpellier. It's not on the way to anywhere. It lies in a closed gorge—remote, tranquil and undisturbed. All that has changed there in centuries is its church cloister. That was bought by George Barnard, a sculptor from Bellefonte, Pa. He shipped it to Manhattan, where it is now one of five of *The* Cloisters in Fort Tyron Park. What an interesting feeling it was to stand in a French mountain church whose principal section of beauty I had already enjoyed in New York.

However, since we are primarily interested in food, I'll spare you surplus geography and driving details and ask you to imagine a happy family assembled beside a brook under rustling sycamores 100 yards from the end of the world. (*La Fin du monde* is the name used by the locals for the meeting place of the gorge walls.) The seats are out of the Deux Chevaux, reposing on thick grass, and the provisions are appearing from the miniscule storage space in the back of the car. I had not assisted with the packing so I had no idea what to expect, except that I knew it was going to be good.

The reason that I had not assisted with the packing (or unpacking) was simply a manifestation of the sharp gender division prevalent in France at the time. It hasn't changed much since. About the main effort Monsieur contributed to the outing was piloting the car, period. The Monsieur telling you this story came close to being thrown out of the house early on in his tutoring career when he suggested after dinner one evening that we men would do the washing up. The three oldest sons and Papa shot me glances that would have stopped the Mistral dead on its tracks. From that time on, I learned not to interfere in matters distaff. I must say that this attitude enhances the pleasures of a French picnic, for males. Sometimes one's conscience has to be ignored.

First, the supply of home-chilled rosé was garnered and placed in the brook to keep its cool. This task went to the younger children, who were only too content to use the occasion for a few moments of happy wading. One bottle, of course, was immediately tapped by us Monsieurs while everybody else scrambled around with blankets and baskets.

A vermillion table cloth the size of a pool table was spread over the flattest area in sight. Dishes and silverware were placed around the edges of the cloth and loaves of bread were put next to Papa. His role at table was not completely passive — there were two tasks which fell unerringly to him, at home or alfresco. He always sliced the bread, after crossing it, and he always tossed the salad. Proper French bread lacks a preservative, (a word that means in French, masculine contraceptive, appropriately enough) and goes rapidly from crisp and tender to hard as a rock throughout. Loaves are therefore cut only as needed. In all fairness, this did keep Papa occupied, as all French persons exhibit an infinite capacity for this staple — at meals and in between. As soon as all the baskets were transferred to the tablecloth, it was time to begin to eat.

While Papa was sawing up the first rounds of bread, Mama and #1 daughter prepared the appetizers. They unwrapped a pâté, slices of *jambon cru* (dark red uncooked country ham), filled a bowl with rich black olives, and opened tins of sardines and mackerel fillets, and started slicing up a large *saucisson*, redolent of garlic which competed nicely with the fresh breezes from the trees. One plate was heaped with a mound of butter and passed around to begin the fun.

I got a big kick out of the French can openers, which are great for picnics. They use large keys like this:

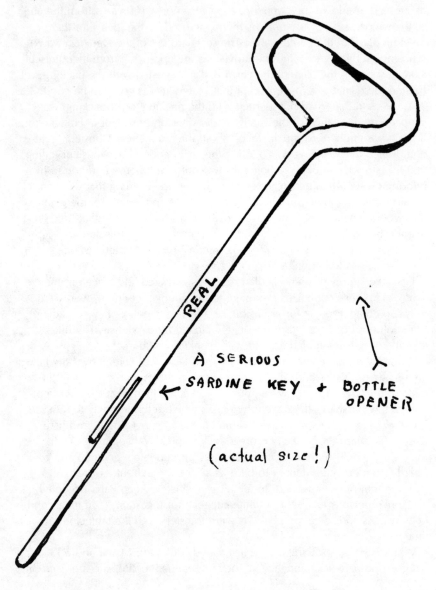

REAL

A SERIOUS
← SARDINE KEY & BOTTLE
OPENER

(actual size!)

Even though the sardines and other tinned things come with those little bitty openers, the French travel with one of these industrial-sized models about 7 inches long sporting a bottle opener on one end and a slot on the other. These keys give powerful leverage on the tin tabs and curtail nasty little skin-ripping incidents that can arise from using less efficient flimsy ones.

For one used to more pedestrian picnics, this splendid array had already assumed banquet proportions. However, it did not take long for the "first" course to vanish, leaving appetites stimulated rather than sated. These tidbits were merely tempters, "Hors d'oeuvres" to be precise. They were followed by two roasts—one veal and the other pink lamb liberally laced with rosemary and slivers of garlic. We daubed slices of these with mustard or mayonnaise and ate them with bread and butter. Mind, these didn't become actual sandwiches. The meat went on our plates and we used our knives and forks, an elegant touch for dining in the rough. Salad was equally elegant and Papa gave it the same treatment he used at home.

At this point, I was ready for a quick gambol about the gorge to help lunch settle down. While Madame and #1 daughter straightened up, the rest of the family and I went exploring. It was hard to believe that there would be more to consume, but there was. On our return we had cheese and more bread and, of course, more rosé.

For a grand finale, we had melons. I'd call them cantaloupes except that that would be damning them with very faint praise. A word association test for the French would elicit *Cavaillon* for "melon" and that's what you'd see on a restaurant menu when the owner wanted you to order one. Cavaillon is a town in the Vaucluse reputed for its melons the way Virginia is for its ham and, alas, imitated in the same manner far from home base. Cavaillon melons are what the gods had in mind when they invented ambrosia. One taste of a good one and you'll swear off all others claiming kinship to the cantaloupe clan. They are small, relatively smooth and thin-skinned, heavy

and brilliantly colored inside. Monsieur had seen to it that there were a half-dozen in the picnic larder. Part of the fun of eating them is comparison tasting. Even though uniformity is not their strong point, *melons de Cavaillon* tend to be delicious even when they aren't at their best!

Lest I ruin your day completely with descriptions of liqueurs and candy and brandied grapes, I'll take leave of our picnic on the grass and join the rest of the family hunting wild mushrooms. That was frequently the last part of an outing before setting out for home. St. Guilhem is not a mushroom paradise so pickings were slim that day. But, for our next picnic, we . . . But that's another story.

9 | recipes that work

Here are some easy recipes for many of the dishes I've been telling you about. Unless otherwise indicated, they will accommodate four to six persons.

If you've ever tried to find out how some cooks do their thing, you've probably encountered the "I put in a pinch of this" and "Oh, I just leave it in the oven until I feel that it's done." That attitude doesn't help much unless the advice is given to someone who is already handy about the kitchen. With that in mind, I have given recipes with quantities and times that have worked for me.

I generally measure things by eye and judge times by look or feel. These notions are hard to communicate, so I suggest that you try the proportions and times I outline. Then, let your instincts take over and change what you think will work better for you on the next go-round.

And now, off to the kitchen . . .

crudités

From page 12

> Raw vegetables such as cabbage, carrots, mirlitons, celery root, etc.
> Mayonnaise and/or French dressing
> Mustard
> Horseradish
> Salt

Grate or shred your choice of vegetables. Add French dressing and mayonnaise. Serve as first course — allow enough to fill a small salad plate per person. Mustard, horseradish and salt optional. Mustard recommended with celery root. Store leftover crudités in refrigerator.

gazpacho

From page 18

> 3 tomatoes
> 1 medium-sized onion
> 1 bell pepper of any color
> 1 cucumber
> 1 quart of tomato juice and/or water
> 1 slice of stale or dry bread
> 2 or 3 cloves of garlic
> Salt & pepper
> ¼ cup of olive oil
> More dry bread for croutons

Cut tomatoes, onion, pepper and cucumber into suitable chunks to use in blender, reserving some of each to dice for use as garnish. Blend these with just enough tomato juice for blender to function. If tomatoes are not in season, use the whole quart of juice. Break up dry bread and add it with garlic, salt, pepper and olive oil to taste. Blend thoroughly. Chill in refrigerator. Serve with garnishes of diced vegetables and croutons.

no-waiting gazpacho

Follow same procedure but use less tomato juice. When ingredients are well blended, add ice cubes, preferably crushed — blend briefly — until ice disappears. Serve as above.

anchovies and endive

From page 14

> 1 tin of flat anchovies per 3 to 4 persons
> 1 Belgian endive per person

Dissolve anchovies in saucepan over medium heat. Put resulting sauce into individual cups on plates, along with one endive for each person. Use endive leaves to scoop up anchovy sauce.

a simple country pâté

From page 19

> ¾ lb. of beef
> ¾ lb. of pork
> ¾ lb. of veal
> 2 whole eggs
> 1 medium-sized onion
> 2 or more cloves of garlic
> ¾ cup of breadcrumbs
> Jigger of cognac
> Milk to moisten bread
> 1 teaspoon of each—dried rosemary, thyme, parsley
> Salt & ground pepper to taste
> Peppercorns
> Salt pork
> One bay leaf

Grind meats together in processor. Add all other ingredients except bay leaf and blend. Place in soufflé-type dish lined with thin slices of salt pork. Stick bay leaf in top. Place dish in pan of water and transfer to 350 degree oven. Bake until done—approximately an hour and a half. Cool before eating—overnight if possible.

For a firmer, dense pâté, place a weight over pâté while it is cooling.

black bean soup

From page 22

> 1¼ pounds of black beans
> 2 medium-sized onions
> 2 stalks of celery
> salt pork
> 1 quart of ham juice from cooking Virginia Ham (Section 4)
> Bay leaves, salt and pepper
> Ham hock (optional)
> 2½ quarts of water

Soak beans in cold water overnight. Chop onions and celery and put them in soup pot at medium heat with enough melted salt pork or bacon grease for them to soften. Plain ham juice can be substituted for fat.

Drain and rinse beans; add to pot of softened onions and celery. Add salt and pepper, one large or two small bay leaves, the ham juice and the water. Put in the ham hock.

Simmer 2 to 3 hours with or without lid. Remove hock and bay leaves. Put through blender, half a container at a time. Mix all blendings.

Serve hot with slices of hard-boiled eggs and thin slices of lemon. Add a teaspoonful or more of medium sherry per bowl, along with a dollop of sour cream.

Accompany with buttered toast and red wine.

emergency spaghetti sauce

From page 24

> **three to four servings**
> 2 medium-sized onions
> ¼ cup of olive oil
> 3 or more cloves of garlic, minced
> A can or jar of *ordinary* commercial spaghetti sauce
> Red wine
> Oregano

Peel and slice onions and cook one of them until black in small quantity of oil. Remove onion slices and pour off oil. Add fresh oil and soften second onion. Add minced garlic, *ordinary* sauce, red wine (about ¼ cup per quart of sauce), and oregano to taste. Put in burnt onion slices. Heat for 10 minutes or more, stirring frequently. Serve with pasta of your choice.

creole court-bouillon

From page 28

2 pounds of fish (avoid oily kind), cut into pieces large enough for individual servings — i.e., about 4 inches in longest dimension.

for marinade

Juice of 1 large lemon or 2 small limes
1 cup of white wine
3 or more mashed cloves of garlic
Salt and pepper
Hot peppers

Mix and use to marinate fish at least 1 hour at room temperature.

ingredients for cooking

Chives
2 medium-sized onions
Tomatoes, fresh or canned
Olive or other cooking oil
White wine
Hot pepper (red)
Juice of ½ lemon
Bouquet garni

Cut up 3 tablespoons of chives and two medium-sized onions and two tomatoes. Cook gently in oil until onions are slightly golden. Pat fish dry with paper towels and add to pot. When both sides of fish are browned, add just enough water to cover pieces and pour in white wine (about half the quantity of water used). Crush red pepper in lemon juice and add along with a bouquet garni. Remove fish when done — 10 minutes or less. Reduce court-bouillon another 5 minutes at high heat. Pour over fish and serve with boiled rice.

blaff   (creole fish soup)

From page 29

> 2 pounds of fish (avoid oily kind), cut into pieces large enough for individual servings — i.e., about 4 inches in longest dimension.
>
> **for marinade**
>
> Juice of 1 large lemon or 2 small limes
> 1 cup of white wine
> 3 or more mashed cloves of garlic
> Salt and pepper
> Hot peppers

Mix and use to marinate fish at least 1 hour at room temperature.

> **ingredients for cooking**
>
> 1 onion
> 3 cloves
> 1 bay leaf
> 2 mashed cloves of garlic
> Bouquet garni
> Fennel (optional)
> Parsley
> Pepper
> White wine
> A lemon or lime

Add cooking ingredients to a quart of water and dry white wine (half and half) and boil gently thirty minutes or more. Add marinated fish and cook for approximately 10 minutes. Squeeze in juice of another lemon and serve as soup.

daube de poissons

From page 31

> 2 pounds of fish — particularly good with fresh tuna. Cut into pieces large enough for individual servings — i.e., about 4 inches in longest dimension.
>
> **for marinade**
>
> Juice of 1 large lemon or 2 small limes
> 1 cup of white wine
> 3 or more mashed cloves of garlic
> Salt and pepper
> Hot peppers

Mix and use to marinate fish at least 1 hour at room temperature.

ingredients for cooking

Flour
Olive or cooking oil
2 onions
Thyme
Chives
Salt and pepper
A lemon or lime

Take fish from marinade, dry and flour pieces and brown quickly in hot oil. Remove fish. In another pan, cook 2 minced onions, pinch of thyme and 2 tablespoons of minced chives plus a little salt and pepper. When onions are golden, add fish, ¼ cup of hot water (not enough to cover fish) and check the seasoning. Cover and let simmer for 10 minutes. Add lemon juice and serve.

acras　　(caribbean cod fritters)

From page 31

¼ lb. of dried codfish
1 medium-sized HOT pepper, cut fine
2 cloves of garlic
4 scallions
3 tablespoons of chopped chives
3 tablespoons of chopped parsley
A pinch of thyme
3 ounces of butter
2 whole eggs
½ cup of milk
1 cup of flour
Salt & pepper

Desalt cod in several changes of water. Chop up together pepper, garlic, scallions, chives and parsley. Use wooden bowl or processor. Add thyme and fish. Continue chopping or processing until thoroughly mixed.

Make a batter of the butter, eggs, milk, flour, salt and pepper. Let the batter sit 3 or 4 hours at room temperature.

When ready to eat, combine batter and fish mixture gently but thoroughly —not by machine. Deep fry tablespoonfuls in hot oil until gold in color. Serve a.s.a.p.

brandade de morue

From page 32

>   1 pound of dried salt codfish
>   3 sprigs of thyme on branches or ½ teaspoon of dried
>   1 bay leaf
>   2 cloves of garlic
>   1 pint of olive oil
>   ¼ cup of sour cream
>   Lemon
>   Pepper

Desalt codfish by soaking it in cold water 6 hours. Change water and soak again 2 more times. Brush off scales if present.

Cut fish in pieces and poach 10 minutes in simmering water with thyme, and bay leaf. Drain fish. When cooled, fish should be flaked and any bones removed.

Crush garlic with cod and add oil slowly to make a paste. If you have a processor, use it here.

Put in heavy pot on low heat and add sour cream slowly. Season with lemon juice and pepper (some salt may be required if desalting was very successful).

Serve hot or cold with boiled potatoes and green salad.

bacalhau d'oiro (golden codfish)

From page 34

>   ½ pound of dried salt codfish
>   3 onions, sliced
>   Olive oil
>   1 pound of potatoes, cut in shoestrings
>   2 eggs

Desalt codfish in several changes of water. Cook sliced onions in olive oil until golden. Add flaked codfish and cook slowly 30 minutes. French fry potatoes while cod is cooking. When potatoes are done, add lightly beaten eggs to cod and onions, leaving heat on. When eggs begin to firm up, gently fold the *hot* French fries into the cod in one or two turns. Serve a.s.a.p.

french-fried *lulas*

From page 36

> A pound of squid per two people
> Lemon juice
> Cooking oil for deep frying
> Flour
> 1 beaten whole egg
> Salt and Pepper

Clean squid and remove head and tentacles. Slice remaining sac into ⅛-inch rings. Marinate in lemon juice an hour or two. Heat oil. Dip rings in flour and then briefly in beaten egg. Fry at 375 degrees 20 to 30 seconds.

lulas recheadas (stuffed squid)

From page 38

> 1 large or two small squid per person — 1½ pounds in all
> 1 cup of milk
> 1 cup of breadcrumbs
> 2 medium-sized onions, minced
> ¼ cup of olive oil
> *Chouriço* — Portuguese sausage — bacon or salt pork if sausage unavailable
> Salt
> ¼ teaspoon of grated nutmeg
> whole egg, slightly beaten
> 2 tomatoes diced finely or in purée
> A teaspoon of Piri-piri
> A cup of dry white wine

Carefully clean squid without breaking sacs. Cut off head and tentacles; chop them fine and put to soak in milk with breadcrumbs. Cook onion in half of olive oil with slices of *chouriço* until sizzling. Add the chopped tentacle and breadcrumb mixture. Add salt if necessary and nutmeg. Remove from heat and stir in slightly beaten egg. When cool enough to handle, stuff this mixture into *lula* sacs ⅔ full and close ends with toothpicks.

Cook chopped onions and tomatoes in olive oil. Add piri-piri and white wine. Place stuffed *lulas* in this mixture and cook slowly for half an hour. Add water if necessary to keep from scorching. Serve with fried potatoes or rice.

cooking oily fish

From page 39

For 2 to 3 pounds of mackerel, tuna or bluefish

baking

Tomatoes, onions, mushrooms, garlic, green peppers
White wine
Herbs of your choice

In a large baking dish, surround fish with vegetables cut into strips and slices. Pour on enough white wine to cover bottom of dish about a quarter of an inch. Sprinkle on herbs. Bake in oven preheated to 400 to 450 degrees. Allow 10 minutes per inch thickness.

easier baking

Mayonnaise and breadcrumbs
Herbs of your choice

Slather both sides of fish with mayonnaise. Sprinkle on breadcrumbs laced with herbs of your choice. Bake in hot oven, 400 to 450 degrees, at 10 minutes to the inch of thickness.

grilling

Plenty of garlic
Herbs

Cut slashes on both sides of fish deep enough to lodge slivers of garlic. Grill over charcoal or equivalent, turning over once. Sprinkle herbs over fish while grilling.

cooking non-oily fish

From page 41

2 to 3 pounds of delicate fish such as flounder, sole, perch, etc.

pan frying

Butter and or olive oil
Seasonings—salt & pepper, an herb you like
Breadcrumbs or instant flour

Heat butter and/or olive oil in frying pan. Salt and pepper fish and coat lightly with breadcrumbs or flour. If herb you select is dried, mix with breadcrumbs or flour. If fresh, drop in pan alongside of fish. Sauté slowly, turning as little as possible—no more than 10 minutes in all for average sized fish.

poaching

1 stalk celery, diced
1 carrot, diced
1 onion, chopped
1 sprig parsely
2 oz. butter
Peppercorns
1 bay leaf
1 clove
1 cup dry white wine
For a little over a quart of court-bouillon, cook celery, carrot, onion and parsley in butter for 2 to 3 minutes. Put this in a quart of water and add 4 or 5 peppercorns, bay leaf, clove and wine. If no wine available, use ⅛ cup of vinegar. Bring to boil and cook gently for at least 15 minutes. Put fish on low rack in pan as close to size of fish as possible. Pour in hot court-bouillon and simmer 10 minutes to the pound. Court-bouillon ideally should be at least 2 inches deep. Remove fish and serve hot or cold with sauce of your choice. Use court-bouillon as base for the sauce or reserve it for fish stock or soup.

steaming

Dry white wine
1 lemon, sliced
Parsely

Place thin fillets of fish in shallow baking dish. Pour in wine to cover bottom of dish to ¼ inch and another ¼ inch of water. Cover with thin slices of lemon and top with fresh chopped parsley. Cover with Saranwrap or equivalent and steam for 10 minutes in a 350 degree oven. In microwave, *recommended*, check at end of 3 minutes on high. If not done, heat more in periods of 30 seconds until it is. Good hot or cold.

beurre blanc

From page 42

> Shallots
> White vinegar
> Butter (½ pound per pound of fish!)
> Salt and pepper if needed

Mince several shallots and put in saucepan with ⅓ cup of white vinegar.
Heat until shallots are reduced to mush. Add more vinegar if necessary.
Using gentle heat, add butter in cubes. Allow each chunk to melt before
adding the next one. When all butter is incorporated, bring mixture to a
bubble and take off burner for fifteen seconds. Repeat, bringing to a bubble
until sauce is thick. Three times should be enough. Do not let boil as butter
could easily separate. Serve a.s.a.p. with fresh water fish if available. *Beurre
blanc* does not do well on reheating.

fish that swim through the door

From page 41

> Assorted fish — heads, bones and all — avoid oily fish such as
> mackerel and blues — allow ½ to ¾ lb. per person

You should have a big catch to make this a gala. Whatever quantity you
have, use these proportions per pound of fish:

> 1 medium-sized onion
> 3 tablespoons of olive oil
> 2 cloves of garlic
> 1 cup of dry white wine
> Pinches of herbs and spices including basil, thyme, fennel and freshly
> ground pepper cayenne pepper, 1 bay leaf
> 2- or 3-inch strip of orange peel, dried or fresh
> 3 fresh tomatoes or half a 15 oz. can of storebought tomato sauce
> Available crustaceans and mollusks not to exceed fish in weight (not
>   counting shells)
> Toasted rough bread
> 2 tablespoons chopped parsley
> Lemon(s)
> Clam juice if you don't make fish stock

Heat sliced onion with olive oil in large pot. When onions are transparent,
put in minced garlic. Add fish heads and bones plus half and half white wine

and water. (Figure half pint of broth per eater when finished.) Add herbs and orange peel. Simmer this while cutting fish into uniform bite-sized pieces.

When bouillon has simmered for half an hour, strain and discard bones, etc. Add tomatoes or sauce. Incorporate and bring to boil. Add fish. After fish has heated 5 minutes, add available clams, mussels and crab or lobster parts. In 10 to 15 minutes *total* time (after fish-laden pot comes to a boil), you're ready to shout "soup's on!" Put pieces of fish on toasted bread, arrange opened shellfish around toast and ladle on broth. Garnish with chopped parsley and serve with lemon wedges.

Warning: prevent over-cooking fish—if it is not all served on first go-round, remove it from pot. The liquid can stay simmering for second servings.

a devil of a fish sauce

From page 44

for four servings

1 stick of butter
Juice of half a big lemon
2 tablespoons of interesting mustard—Dijon type, for example
2 tablespoons of fresh chopped chives
2 tablespoons of fresh chopped parsley
Cayenne pepper to suit the eaters

Soften the butter and add the above ingredients in order. Use as much pepper as you can without upsetting guests. Spread this mixture on hot broiled fish directly as it leaves the heat. Serve at once.

bifteck à l'hélène

From page 47

for two persons

1/4 lb. of butter
Small head of garlic
One lemon or 2 limes
Fresh ground pepper
Chopped parsley
1 lb. of inexpensive steak—sliced thin
Cooking oil of your choice or more butter

On large metal plate put butter, minced cloves from the whole head of garlic, juice from lemon or limes, ground pepper and chopped parsley. Place close enough to source of heat to make butter soften but NOT cook.

In a frying pan cook steak slices in oil or butter. Cook both sides over high heat until done to your preference. As they become ready, put steaks directly on mound of ingredients on warm plate. Turn slices over to coat thoroughly and serve. Butter should melt from heat of meat—if not, help it along with very low flame, being careful not to cook garlic.

pollo al ajillo (garlic chicken)

From page 48

for two persons
1 small chicken
Salt & pepper
¼ cup of olive oil
20 + cloves of garlic
¼ cup of medium sherry

Chicken can be uncooked or leftover stewed, roasted or barbequed.

Cut chicken into equally sized morsels 1½ to 2 inches a side. Salt and pepper them. Heat large frying pan and put in oil and 2 cloves of garlic slivered. Remove garlic as soon as it starts to color. Sauté chicken pieces until done—about 10 to 15 minutes. (If chicken has been previously cooked, just get it hot.)

Remove chicken and replace with at least 20 cloves of sliced garlic. Heat gently until garlic is soft. Put chicken back in. Turn up the heat. As soon as garlic begins to turn golden, pour on the sherry. Rock the pan until sherry is well distributed. When it bubbles, tilt the pan just enough to let stove ignite it. Serve as soon as flame dies out. The ideal accompaniment is French-fried potatoes.

When using an electric stove, you may prefer to use a match—for safety (and cleaning-up after) reasons.

poulet à l'ail (garlic chicken)

From page 50

for two to three persons
Salt & pepper
6 chicken thighs or other pieces
2 tsps. of cooking oil
⅛ lb. of butter (½ stick)
20 cloves of garlic
½ cup of dry white wine
1½ cups of hot milk
1 tbsp. of cornstarch
½ cup of sour cream
Juice of 1 lemon

Use a heavy casserole with lid. Salt and pepper chicken and brown it at high heat in the oil and all but a tablespoon of the butter.

When chicken is uniformly golden, turn down heat, cover pan and simmer for 10 minutes.

Peel and mash garlic cloves. Remove chicken to warm place and put garlic and the rest of butter in the pot. Stir constantly with wooden spoon over low heat until garlic softens and begins to stick to spoon. Add wine and bring to boil for 3 minutes.

Put chicken back in pan. Pour in hot milk and cover. Simmer.

While chicken is simmering, mix cornstarch thoroughly into sour cream. Add some of cooking liquid to sour cream and cornstarch to make a uniform mixture and pour it into the pot after chicken is cooked — about 15 minutes. Turn up heat. After bubbles appear, continue high heat for 3 minutes, stirring to prevent burning. Serve with rice and/or crusty bread. Squeeze on lemon juice as desired.

piri-piri (hot pepper sauce)

From page 51

6 to 8 small hot peppers
½ pint of olive oil
1 thick slice of lemon with rind
1 large bay leaf

Split open peppers and put them in a glass receptacle which can be sealed air-tight. Add oil, lemon slice and bay leaf. Seal and store at room temperature for at least three weeks before using.

a proper curry

From page 55

Proportions are not given here—curry is a use-up-what-you-have-on-hand dish, so anything goes.

> Onions and garlic
> Olive or other cooking oil
> Meat or fish (not both)
> Cornstarch
> Bell peppers
> Fresh ginger, slivered
> Carrots
> Apple, sliced
> Curry powder
> Diverse leftovers
> Wine
> Coconut and coconut milk
> Lemon

trimmings (any or all of the following):

> Diced onions, peppers, almonds, peanuts, cashews, tomatoes
> Lemon and/or lime wedges
> Sliced bananas
> Ginger
> Burnt onions
> Raisins
> Hard-boiled eggs cut into pieces
> Sliced cucumbers in yoghurt with cumin
> Sour cream with fresh grated ginger
> Bombay Duck
> Poppadums
> Anything else you can think of to munch with this meal

Fry onions and garlic in oil until golden and remove from pan.

Dust meat or fish with cornstarch and brown in remaining oil. Add more oil if needed.

Remove meat or fish and replace with peppers, slivers of fresh ginger, carrots, apple slices and an initial spoonful of curry. Add more oil if needed and any leftover vegetables you want to use up.

Cook 10 minutes over medium heat and return meat to pan. (Fish should be added later in the process than meat).

Add a cup of undistinguished wine. Put in two more spoonfuls of curry.
Add shredded coconut, coconut milk and a lemon half. Simmer for a quarter
of an hour and taste. Add more curry if needed.

Start preparing trimmings. Burn onions black and dice and slice vegetables.
Put sliced cucumber with yoghurt and cumin in refrigerator.

One hour is enough for flavors to meld but cooking may continue so long
as you remember to add liquid when necessary—wine or water.

Twenty minutes before serving, put water to boil for rice. Fifteen minutes
before serving, put rice in boiling water and add fish to curry.

Five minutes before rice is done, heat oil for poppadums and begin
"popping" them.

When rice is done, drain and put portions on plates. Ladle curry over rice.
Put trimmings on table and let everyone self-serve.

This is a flexible concoction. The basic ingredients are meat or fish, curry
and onions with some kind of oil. The more of the other ingredients you can
muster, the more exciting will be the finale. Serve with chilly beer or nondescript cold wine.

virginia ham

From page 59

> 1 Virginia ham
> 2 bay leaves
> ¼ cup black molasses
> ½ cup cider vinegar
> Brown sugar
> Bread crumbs
> Dry mustard
> Ground cloves

Scrub ham with brush and soak in cold water overnight. Pour off water. Put
ham in large vessel, SKINSIDE DOWN, and cover with fresh water. Heat—
preferably in oven. When water simmers, add bay leaves, molasses and
vinegar. Cook about 25 minutes per pound at 180 degrees. Add water to
keep ham covered as needed but do not let it boil.

When done, remove from vessel and take off skin while ham is still warm
(SAVE juice for other recipes.) Cover skinned side with mixture of brown
sugar, bread crumbs, dry mustard and ground cloves. Use cloves sparingly—
½ teaspoon at most. Place in hot oven until brown. Watch carefully after 10
minutes as covering can scorch quickly.

Cool before slicing. Cut from small end first.

iscas — liver portuguese style

From page 63

2 lbs. of liver—beef, calf or pig sliced thin

for the marinade:

2 or 3 cloves of garlic
1 cup of hearty red wine
A jigger of vinegar (1-2 oz.)
Salt and pepper
A pinch of dried thyme (or 2 sprigs of fresh)
1 bay leaf
A dash of olive oil for rubbing the *iscas*

Crush garlic and mix with other marinade ingredients. Slice liver and rub with olive oil. Place slices, one at a time, in glass dish. Cover with marinade. Let stand at room temperature at least two hours, turning slices over from time to time.

for final preparation

¼ lb. of bacon
3 tbsps. of olive oil
Parsley

Fry bacon in olive oil and remove to drain. Dry liver pieces with paper towels and brown 2 minutes to a side in hot bacon fat and oil. Take liver out and keep it warm. Pour marinade in frying pan and heat vigorously until half evaporated. Pour over liver and crumble bacon on top. Garnish with parsley. Serve with boiled or fried potatoes.

chicken liver surprise

From page 64

for two to three persons

Chicken livers (one pound)
3 tablespoons of butter
3 tablespoons of flour (Wondra preferred)
¾ cup of chicken stock or broth (real or from bouillon cubes)
10 to 12 ounces of noodles or pasta of your choice

1 tablespoon of olive oil
Salt and pepper
Rosemary and/or thyme
2 cloves of garlic
2 or 3 tablespoons of medium sherry
½ cup of sour cream
Parsley

Put pot of water on for pasta.

Clean livers carefully and pat dry with paper towel.

Prepare a roux of part of the butter and flour—equal quantities of each. Stir roux into pint of stock or bouillon and let it thicken. Stir frequently.

Put the pasta in the pot to cook—note time.

Sauté livers in olive oil and the rest of the butter. Season with salt and pepper, thyme and rosemary. Squeeze in garlic. Add sherry and slosh around pan. When livers are done enough to suit you, pour juices from sauté pan into stock and stir well. Add sour cream and heat to bubbling.

Drain pasta. Make individual portions and place livers on top. Pour sauce over and garnish with parsley.

interesting green peas

From page 66

for three to four persons

1 very small finely minced onion
2 tablespoons of butter
1 tablespoon of breadcrumbs
10 oz. package of smallest frozen green peas or equivalent of canned or fresh
1 pinch of sugar

Lightly sauté minced onion in butter until translucent. Mix in 1 tablespoon of breadcrumbs and pinch of sugar. When breadcrumbs have absorbed most of the butter, put in peas, unthawed. Heat until peas are hot.

If using canned peas, drain and add same way as frozen. Heat until warm enough to eat.

If garden-fresh, add peas to onions, butter and breadcrumbs with small amount of water (2 tablespoons) to keep from burning. Cook until tender but still firm. Sugar may be omitted.

artichokes & steamed anything

From page 69

use a stainless steel or glass vessel

Artichokes (or other vegetables to be steamed)
Water

Prepare artichokes by trimming leaf ends approximately ½ inch. Trim off dry part of stems. Strip off any dry leaves from bottom.

For young small artichokes, trimming is not necessary except for stem ends.

TO STEAM: Place stem down in basket or trivet over boiling water. Steam until fork enters stems easily. Time depends on size and age of artichokes and can go from 10 to 45 minutes. Drain upside down so that excess water will run off.

TO BOIL: Place in boiling water until artichokes pass fork test. Drain upside down.

general steaming rule:

From page 69

Cut vegetables such as cauliflower, broccoli, squash, etc., into small pieces as close to same size as possible. Put on rack or trivet above water and steam *only* until knife or fork will penetrate pieces with little resistance. Steamer with lid on requires slightly less time.

ratatouille provençale

From page 75

1½ lbs. of eggplant
2 lbs. of courgettes (zucchini)
¼ lb. of onions
3 cloves of garlic
1½ lbs. of bell peppers
1¼ lbs. of tomatoes
3 ounces (fluid) of olive oil
4 ounces (fluid) of water
Salt and pepper

Peel the eggplant, zucchini, onions and garlic. Wash the other vegetables. Slice everything in pieces about a third of an inch thick and put in a pot. Pour on the olive oil and add the water. Simmer for 2 hours, covered. Crush the results and serve hot or cold. Salt and pepper to taste.

george's *ratatouille*

From page 76

Soften the onions in hot oil. Don't peel the eggplant. Skip the zucchini.
Leave out the water. Add large pinches of rosemary and thyme. Everything
else is the same.

philadelphia fried tomatoes

From page 77

for two to three persons

Firm tomatoes (about 6)
Salt and pepper
Sugar (light brown if possible)
Flour
Butter
Milk
Bacon (optional)

Slice tomatoes in ⅓-inch rounds. Salt and pepper slices, sprinkle small pinch
of sugar on each (more if unripe), coat with flour and fry in butter until
brown on both sides. Remove all but two slices of tomatoes from pan to
warm place. Mash the two slices of tomato in pan. Add roux of 1 tablespoon
each of butter and flour. When roux is well heated and smooth, pour in ⅔
cup of hot milk. Continue heating and stirring until thick. Pour over tomatoes
and serve.

Bacon drippings can be used in place of butter for initial frying. Pour off fat
before adding roux to slices mashed for gravy. Serve with bacon rashers and
pan gravy.

tomatoes à *la provençale*

From page 76

for two to three persons

6 tomatoes
¼ cup of olive oil
¾ cup of breadcrumbs
3 or more cloves of garlic, minced
Thyme
Rosemary or oregano

Slice tomatoes in ⅓-inch rounds. Make paste of oil, breadcrumbs, garlic and herbs. Spread on one side of tomato slices. Place in lightly oiled broiler pan. Broil five to ten minutes far enough from burner to prevent topping from burning.

Substitute oregano for rosemary and/or thyme according to preference.

zucchini at its best

From page 74

for three to four persons
Zucchini (1 lb.)
½ stick of butter
Juice of ½ lemon
3 tablespoons of chopped fresh dill or 1 teaspoon of dill weed
½ cup of sour cream
Salt and pepper

Slice unpeeled zucchini into thin rounds about ⅛-inch thick. Sauté them quickly in hot butter for about a minute. While slices are still firm, moisten with lemon juice. Sprinkle on chopped dill or dried dill weed. Add sour cream and stir over heat just long enough for cream to warm. Salt and pepper to taste. Serve as soon as possible.

josé's non-lumpy mashed potatoes

From page 85

2 pounds of potatoes
½ pint of milk
Salt and pepper
1 stick (4 oz.) of butter

Peel potatoes and cut into same size pieces. Put them in boiling water. Check for tenderness with knife at end of 15 minutes. Remove and drain when knife enters easily and comes out clean. Heat milk.

Put hot potatoes in bowl of electric mixer and start it at slow speed. Add a pinch of salt and butter cut into chunks. When butter melds with potatoes, add hot milk *very* gradually with mixer still going. Keep speed slow to avoid sloshing milk out of bowl. When potatoes look creamy, speed up briefly and serve. (Not all the milk may be required—quantity depends on how watery potatoes are.)

leftover-mashed-potato pancakes

From page 85

> Leftover mashed potatoes
> Onions, finely cut
> Butter
> Cooking oil (olive or other)
> Salt and pepper

Non-stick pan *highly* recommended.

Let potatoes get firm in the refrigerator. Make round cakes of the mashed potatoes about 3 inches across and ½ inch thick. Brown onions in butter and a little oil in largest frying pan handy. Take out half the onions. Place the cakes on top of onions in pan and put rest of onions on top of cakes. Fry over medium heat until onions and potato form a crisp "skin." Turn once *carefully* and brown other side. 2 minutes per side should be enough. Salt and pepper to taste. Serve for breakfast, alone or with eggs, or as a side dish with another meal.

josé's *tortilla española*

From page 86

> **Per person:**
>
> 2 medium-sized potatoes
> 2 tablespoons of olive oil
> Salt and pepper
> 1 small onion
> 1 Bell pepper—any color
> 1 egg

Cut potatoes in "shoelace" strips or thin slices. Fry these quickly in olive oil with a small amount of salt. Fry sliced onion and pepper in oil with salt and pepper—preferably in another pan. When potatoes are done enough to eat as is, mix in onion and pepper and pour at least one beaten egg on top of mixture. Lift edge to let eggs run underneath, forming tortilla. Flip, using second pan as top if necessary. Cook until egg appears done and serve hot. (Also makes good *macho* lunch-box sandwich to be eaten cold.)

nicerice

From page 87

(This is for fluffy rice.)

for two to four persons
1 cup of rice — long-grained
3 cups of water
Saffron or achiote (optional)

Bring water to a boil. Add coloring (ground *achiote* or saffron) to water if desired. Add Rice. Boil for 15 minutes. Remove from heat and add 2 cups of cold water. Drain immediately and serve.

If not convenient to serve at once, rice may be kept fluffy by leaving it in colander or strainer over bubbling water.

super-rich mayonnaise

From page 108

6 egg yolks
1 tsp. salt
2 tbsps. Vinegar (tarragon-flavored preferred)
1 pint of salad oil
1 tsp. dry mustard
Worcestershire sauce
1 lemon

With ingredients at same (room) temperature, put egg yolks in mixing bowl and beat at high speed. Add salt and vinegar. Start adding oil VERY slowly. When half the oil has been added and mayonnaise has formed, add mustard and Worcestershire. Continue adding oil at faster pace. If mayonnaise is very stiff before all oil is put in, add juice of lemon. Otherwise, add at end. Taste and add more of any of the seasoning if necessary. Beat in a tablespoon or two of boiling water at very end if mayonnaise is not going to be used right away.

Note: More oil can be used for a "lighter" mayonnaise.

blender mayonnaise

From page 109

Use ⅓ of ingredients listed above plus ¼ to ½ cup more oil. Instead of 2 yolks, use 1 whole egg and 1 yolk. Put in eggs, salt, mustard and vinegar at beginning. When blended, add oil slowly. When mixture coagulates, add rest of oil as fast as it can be absorbed. If mayonnaise turns solid, stop blender, scrape down sides with rubber spatula and add lemon juice to soften. Continue with oil until all is used.

processor mayo

From page 109

Follow blender method (at slow speed) but use only yolks. Taste is slightly different without whites.

aunt bertha's american french dressing

From page 109

To make around a quart, put the following into a blender:

> 1 small onion, cut up
> ½ cup powdered sugar
> 1 tbsp. paprika
> ⅛ red pepper (cayenne)
> 1 tbsp. dry mustard
> ¾ tsp. salt
> ½ cup tarragon vinegar
> ½ cup cider vinegar
> 1 pint of mild salad oil (not olive)
> 1 egg white (optional)

Blend and bottle—keep in refrigerator. Shake before using.
   Optional egg white may be added to help keep dressing from separating, but may make it difficult to pour.

pie crust — "southern" pastry

From page 117

For one 9-inch pie, covered, or two 9-inch shells:

> 2 cups of sifted all-purpose flour
> ½ tsp. salt
> 1 cup of shortening — ⅓ butter, ⅔ Crisco
> 6 tbsps. ice water

Put the sifted flour and salt into a mixing bowl and work in the shortening gently but thoroughly with your fingers. Add water a little at a time. Work into a ball, dust with flour and put in refrigerator for ¾ of an hour.

If using a food processor, dump all ingredients in together and knead only until uniform but no longer. Refrigerate.

Pre-heat oven.

Divide into two hunks. Roll and fit into pie tin(s). For empty pie shell, bake at 450 degrees for 10 to 12 minutes.

For filled pie shells: pre-heat oven to 425 degrees and bake for 10 minutes. Reduce heat to 350 and cook for time suggested by particular filling recipe you are following— ½ hour plus.

vinegar pie crust

From page 120

For two 9-inch pie crusts tops and bottoms.

part one

4 cups of sifted all-purpose flour
½ cup of water
1⅓ cups of shortening—(1 part butter to 2 parts Crisco or similar)

part two

1 whole egg
2 tsps. salt
1 tbsp. plain white vinegar

If doing this by hand, mix parts one and two separately. Then combine the two and knead into a ball. Put it into a refrigerator for at least ½ hour before rolling out.

If using a food processor: put all ingredients in machine and mix until uniform but no longer. Refrigerate before rolling.

When baking, proceed as in "Southern" pastry.

old-fashioned vinegar pies

From page 120

pie #1

1 cup of *mild* vinegar
1 cup of water
1 tbsp. butter
1½ tbsps. flour
⅔ cup of sugar

Combine ingredients and heat until they are dissolved. Add cold water and stir over heat until thick.

Pour into pie crust and bake for 15 minutes at 350 degrees or until firm.

pie #2

1 egg
1 cup of sugar
1½ tbsps. flour
1 cup of cold water
1 tbsp. vinegar
Dash of grated nutmeg

Beat (vigorously) egg, sugar and flour together. Stir in rest of ingredients and bake in crust as above.

Both pies will be greatly enhanced by meringues. Spoon 2 stiffly beaten egg whites and ½ cup of sugar over top of pie after the 15 minute baking time and return to oven long enough to set meringue and turn it slightly golden.

Food coloring added to filling makes these more attractive pies—try light green.

cherry pie

From page 118

For a 9-inch pie

One No. 2 can of sour cherries
½ cup of sugar
A pinch of salt
1 tbsp. melted butter
2½ tablespoons of tapioca
⅛ tsp. almond extract
2 tbsps. lemon juice

Pre-heat oven to 450 degrees.

Mix all of the ingredients together.

Use either Southern or Vinegar pie crust—see two preceding recipes.

Roll out pastry and line bottom of pie pan. Fill pan and cover with plain circle of dough or a lattice of strips of dough. If using solid circle, make holes for steam to escape. Place in oven for 10 minutes at 450 degrees. Reduce heat to 350 and bake approximately ½ hour.

apple crumble

From page 121

for three to four persons

1 cup flour
1 cup dark brown sugar
1 stick (4 oz.) butter
2 large apples
lemon juice
⅛ to ¼ cup white sugar
½ tsp. cinnamon
A small piece of lemon peel

method

Mix flour and brown sugar. Cut softened butter (not melted) into chunks and use your fingers to work them into flour and sugar to produce a crumbly mixture.

Slice apples and put them into baking dish or pan. Sprinkle lemon juice over apples. Dust with white sugar, the amount depending on how sour the apples are—(⅛ to ¼ of a cup). Distribute cinnamon over top, lemon peel in center.

Cover the apple slices with the crumble mixture, trying to cover whole surface if possible. Bake 20 minutes in oven pre-heated to 300 degrees. If juice is bubbling and crumble is golden, it's ready.

other fruit crumbles

From page 121

When made with other fruits—adjust white sugar and lemon juice to correspond to sourness. Rhubarb, for example, needs more white sugar and less lemon juice.

easy meringues

From page 121

6 egg whites
Cream of tartar
1½ cups of sugar (granulated or finer)
Shredded coconut (optional)

Whip egg whites until firm in scrupulously clean bowl. Add a pinch of cream of tartar. Remove bowl from mixer and gently fold in sugar (and coconut if you choose). Ladle tablespoonfuls onto non-stick cookie sheet or brown paper on regular cookie sheet. Bake at under 200 degrees until they resist finger pressure. When cool, store in air-tight container.

BETTER BET: Meringues can be put in recently used warm oven and left overnight with heat turned off.

macaroons

From page 123

> 6 egg whites
> Cream of tartar
> 1½ cups of sugar (granulated or finer)
> Shredded coconut and/or almonds

Proceed as with meringues. Whip egg whites until firm in scrupulously clean bowl. Add a pinch of cream of tartar. At low speed, mix in sugar. As soon as sugar is distributed, stop beater. Use a large spoon and fold in by hand 1 cup of shredded coconut and/or ½ cup of pulverized almonds. Ladle table-spoonfuls onto non-stick cookie sheet or brown paper on regular cookie sheet. Bake at 300 degrees for 30 minutes or until they resist finger pressure. When cool, store in air-tight container.

virginia fried apples

From page 123

per person
> 4 to 5 rashers of bacon
> 2 to 3 firm, tart apples
> Brown sugar
> White sugar if apples are very sour
> Water or white wine

Cook bacon slowly in largest frying pan available.

Cut up unpeeled apples into pieces—none thicker than ½ inch. Replace bacon with apples in the bacon drippings. (Pour off some of drippings if bacon is very fat.) Cook a few minutes, stirring, and sprinkle on brown sugar. (Add some white sugar if apples are sour.) Continue frying. Stir frequently and mash apples as they become soft. Add water or wine if necessary to keep apples from burning.

When apples offer little resistance to stirring implement, they are done. Serve with buttered toast and the bacon.

if you are in a hurry

Cut up apples as above. Mix in brown sugar and pour on a quarter of a cup of water or white wine. Cut bacon rashers into 2-inch lengths and put on top of apples. Place in microwave and heat on high. Use browning element along with microwave heat. At end of 5 minutes, remove bacon, stir apples and heat 5 more minutes.

Finish cooking the bacon in a frying pan. Remove bacon. Finish apples by frying and mashing in pan—about another 3 to 5 minutes.

cornmeal pancakes

From page 126

for two to three persons

1 cup of cornmeal, water-ground if you can find it
1½ cups of milk
1½ tsps. sugar
¼ tsp. salt
¼ tsp. baking powder
1 egg
2 tbsps. of melted butter

Soak cornmeal 2 minutes in heated milk. Mix dry ingredients. Beat in egg and melted butter. Combine with cornmeal and milk. Batter will look thin but don't worry—it works.

Stir each time you drop tablespoonfuls on medium hot griddle. When bubbles stop forming, flip once. Cakes should be light gold in color and lacy. Serve as you would ordinary pancakes.

easy does it spoonbread

From page 127

for three to four persons

2 cups of water
1 cup of cornmeal
1 tbsp. butter
1 tsp. salt
2 cups of milk
4 eggs
2 tsps. baking powder

Preheat oven to 425 degrees.

Boil water and put cornmeal in it to soak. Leave on low heat. While meal is swelling up, stir in the butter and salt. Remove pan from stove.

When slightly cooled, mix in milk, eggs and baking powder. Bake for around 25 minutes in a bowl you can use at the table. Serve it HOT.

quick *crêpes*

From page 115

for two to three persons

¾ cup of milk
⅓ cup of instant (Wondra) flour
1 egg
⅛ tsp. of salt
1 tsp. sugar
3 tbsps. of melted butter

Mix ingredients together adding butter last. Or put everything into blender and whip a few seconds.

Pour small amount into heated non-stick pan and swirl to cover bottom of pan. (One tablespoon will do for 5- to 6-inch pan.) When top of *crêpe* is no longer shiny, flip and do other side briefly. (It may be necessary to loosen edge with plastic spatula—when *crêpe* slides easily, it's time to flip.) Remove to another plate. Put pat of butter on each while still warm. Sprinkle with sugar and lemon juice or spread with jelly or jam. Roll up and serve.

If *crêpes* are too gummy for your taste, add a tablespoon of flour to batter.

bananes flambées

From page 29

½ dozen bananas
½ cup of butter
½ cup light brown sugar
½ cup of rum

Peel bananas. Slice in half lengthwise and place in a pan that can go under broiler. Melt butter and cover bananas. Broil for 5 minutes and pour sugar over bananas. Broil another 2 minutes, far enough from flame so that sugar will not burn. Heat rum and pour over broiled bananas. Light with match and jump out of the way. Last step most effective at table but everything must be HOT.

This can be done without a broiler in a large frying pan. In this case, put sugar on at beginning.

pão-de-ló

From page 128

> 1 cup of honey
> 1 cup of olive oil
> 1 cup of sugar
> 7 egg yolks
> 1 tsp baking powder
> Nutmeg
> 2½ cups of flour
> 7 egg whites
>
> (And—enough nerve to try this out!)

Bring honey and oil to a boil. Set aside to cool. When lukewarm, add to it a cup of sugar that has been beaten into 7 egg yolks. Sift baking powder and nutmeg with 2½ cups of flour and add to egg mixture. Gently fold in beaten egg whites. Bake in greased tin for 45 minutes at 330 degrees.

Use a tin with at least 2-inch sides. This cake should be higher than a regular layer cake.

general index

bold numbers refer to real cooking recipes in back of book

banana, chiquita, 80
breads
  churros, 100
  corn cakes, 126–127, **170**
  pão-de-ló, 100, 128, **172**
  papsecos, 4
  poppadums, 56–57
  real, 107
  spoon bread, 127–128, **170**
chicken
  pollo al ajillo, 48–49, **154**
  poulet à l'ail, 50–51, **155**
  volaille de bresse à la crème, 8
child, julia, 44, 102, 119
curry
  ingredients, 106
  making one, 56–57, **156–157**
cynarin, 73
deighton, len, 3
desserts
  bananes flambées, 29, **171**
  cherry pie, 118–119, **167**
  crêpes, 115, **171**
  crumbles, apple and other fruit, 121, **168**
  flan, 90
  macaroons, 123, **169**
  meringues, 121–123, **168, 169**
  pie crust, "southern pastry," 117, 118, **165–166**
  pie crust, vinegar, 120, **166**
diller, phyllis, 19
eggs
  as in english breakfast, 74
  boiling of, 17–18
  in golden codfish, *bacalhau d'oiro*, 34, **148**
  josé's tortilla, 86, **163**
  omelet with *brandade de morue*, 34

  whites, how to use up, 121–123, **168, 169**
  with cape cod turkey, 35
fish, see also seafood dishes
  bluefish, 39
  catfish, 9
  cod, 31–36
  mackerel, 39
  non-oily fish preparations, 41
  oily fish preparations, 39–41
  pike, 43
  poaching, **151**
  sardines, 40
  scrod versus schrod, 35
  shad, 43
  steaming, 44, **151**
  trout, 8
  tuna, 39
flambe
  bananes flambées, 29, **171**
  pollo al ajillo, 49, **154**
fruits
  ahuacatl, 15
  alligator pears, 15
  apples, southern fried, 123–126, **169–170**
  avocado, 14–15
  mangoes, how to get ripe ones, 80
  melons de cavaillon, 139
  oranges, green but ripe!, 79
  ugli, 79
garlic
  aphrodisiac (conditional), 93
  chicken dishes, 48–51, **154–155**
  festival in gilroy, 94
  for spaghetti, 24
  garlic lovers cookbook, 94
  gilroy, 92–93
  in grilled fish, 39

garlic (*cont.*)
  in just about all of section 4, 46–65
  in lamb, 139
  in pâté, 21, **143**
  in *provençale* preparations, 75–76,
    160–162
  with oily fish, 40, **150**
gouveia, jose, 96
guilhem, saint, 136, 140
ham
  genuine smithfield, 58
  jambon cru, 58
  presunto de chaves, 58
  prosciutto, 58
  serrano, 58
  virginia, 57–60
  virginia, boiling and baking, 59, **157**
  virginia, buying by mail, 60
  with oysters and corn cakes, 127
herbs & spices
  achiote, 89
  annatto, 89
  bois d'inde, 30
  chart of suggested uses, 103–105
  cloves, 101
  cloves when glazing virginia ham,
    59
  comparison, 101
  cumin in curry, 106
  dried versus fresh, 102
  ginger, 13, 56
  jamaican pepper, 30
  oregano freaks, 101
  oregano with string beans, 68
  piment, 28
  roucou, 29
  saffron, 89
  tarragon in vinegar, 110
hot stuff
  blaff, 29–30, **146**
  capsicum, 55
  coleman's mustard, 13
  piri-piri, 28–29, 39, 51–53, **155**
kitchen gadgets
  a superb can and bottle opener,
    138–139
  caldeira, 39
  coccotte minute, 89
  disposal (warning about), 72

  fogareiro, 3, 4
  micro-wave, 86, 125–126
  mouli-julienne, 12, 84, 86
  pressure cooker, 39, 89–91
  terrine, 20, 21
  turbo-oven, 45, 120
  wooden spoon advantage, 51
mackenzie, donald, 3
meats
  bifteck à l'hélène, 47–48, **153–155**
  chicken livers, 64–65, **158–159**
  chorizo, 38
  chouriço, 38
  filetes, 113
  foie de veau grillé, 63
  foie gras, 20
  iscas de porco, 63–64, **158**
  linguiça, 4, 38
  marinating of, 61–62
  pâté, 19–22, **143**
  pseudo-sauerbraten, 131
  saddle of hare and how to prepare,
    130–131
  spiced round, 9
  tamale, 134–135
o conde de marim y alte, 3
olive oil
  classification, 95
  cooking with, 99–100
  in salad, 99
  oleic acid, 95
  proper storing, 96
  wholesale source, 96
olives
  californian, 98
  oleuropein, 99
  types of, 98–99
  uses besides food, 96
parmentier, antoine, 81
pasta
  spaghetti, 24–26
  with chicken livers, 64–65, **158–159**
perdue, frank, 50
potatoes
  baked, 86
  french-frying, 81
  home made chips, 83
  josé's non-lumpy mashed, 85, **162**
  josé's spanish tortilla, 86, **163**

leftover mashed, what to do with, 85
microwaved, 86
pommes de terre soufflées, 85
waxy versus mealy, 82–83
raleigh, sir walter, 81
ratatouille, 75–76, **160–161**
rice
  cooking rule of thumb, 87–88
  fluffy versus gummy (nicerice), 87,
    164
  indian, 88
  japanes, 88
rijsttafel, 55
salad dressing
  aunt bertha's american-french, 109–
    110, **165**
  mayonnaise, 107–109, **164–165**
  vinaigrette, 109
salads
  anchovy and endive, 14, **143**
  celeri remoulade, 13
  crudités, 12–13, **142**
  simple, 99, 112
  szechuan cabbage, 13
sandwiches
  fantastic onion, 110
  mustard butter spread for, 60
  virginia ham spread for, 60
  world's greatest tunafish, 53
sauces
  anchovy (for endive), 14, **143**
  beurre blanc, 42–44, **152**
  devil (for fish), 44–45, **153**
  gahuacamolli, 15
  mole, 15
  piri-piri (see spicy things)
  roux, 65, 114
  spaghetti, emergency, 24–26, **144**
Seafood dishes
  acras, 31–32, **147**
  bacalhau d'oiro, gold-plated cod,
    34, **148**
  blaff de poissons, 29–30, **146**
  brandade de morue, 32–34, **148**
  calamari—see *lulas*, 36–38
  caldeirada of lulas, 39
  cape cod turkey, 35
  curried fish, 55–56
  daube de poissons, 31, **146–147**

fish that swim through the door, 41–
  42, **152–153**
le vrai court-bouillon, 28–29, **145**
lulas, french fried, 36, **149**
lulas recheadas, 38, **149**
lulas and rice, 37–38
squid—see *lulas*, 36–38
truite farçies braisées au porto, 8
smith, granny, 125
smith, jeff, 65
soups
  black bean, 22–24, **144**
  blaff, 29–30, **146**
  court-bouillon, 28–29, **145**
  gazpacho, 18–19, **142**
  gazpacho del rio, 19
  kidney bean, lentil & split pea, 23–
    24, 90, 91
  potage parmentière, 81
  stock made with pressure cooker, 90
spicy things
  beurre rouge, 29
  bombay duck, 56
  chutney, 80
  colorau, 4, 37
  curry powder ingredients, 106
  horseradish, 13
  mustard as *celeri* tenderizer, 13
  piri-piri, 28–29, 39, 51–53, **155**
  polluelos, 89
  poudre de colombo, 106
  ramolas, 13
  soy sauce, 13
  szechuan cabbage, 13
umberto, signor, 107
vegetables
  artichokes, 69–72, **160**
  broccoli, 68
  cabbage, 13
  carrots, 13
  cauliflower, 67–68
  celeriac, 13
  chayotes, 13
  chouchoutes, 13
  christophines, 13
  courgettes, 75
  cucumbers, 13
  eggplant, 75–76
  jerusalem artichokes, 73

vegetables (*cont.*)
  mirlitons, 13
  onions to make green peas interest-
    ing, 67, **159**
  onions, race-track tratment, 26
  peas, interesting green, 66–67, **159**
  potatoes—listed separately, 80–86
  radishes, 13
  rice—listed separately, 87–89
  shallots in *beurre blanc*, 43, **152**
  tomatoes, 74–78, **161–162**
  turnips, 13
  zucchini, 74–78, **162**

vinegar
  alegar, 111
  as tenderizer, 113–114
  flavored, making your own, 112–
    113
  grains to measure strength, 111
  malt, with fish & chips, 111
  used in boiling eggs, 18
  used in pie and pie crust, 120, **166–
    167**
  with potatoes, 100
wondra flour, 65, 115

real recipes

real cooking recipes and where to find them

acras, caribbean cod fritters, **147**
anchovies and endive, **143**
artichokes and steamed anything, **160**
bacalhau d'oiro, golden codfish, **148**
bananes flambées, **171**
beurre blanc, **152**
bifteck à l'hélène, **153–154**
black bean soup, **144**
blaff, creole fish soup, **146**
brandade de morue, **148**
chicken liver surprise, **158–159**
corn cakes, cornmeal pancakes, **170**
creole court-bouillon, **145**
crêpes, **171**
crudités, **142**
crumble, apple or other fruits, **168**
curry, **156-157**
daube de poissons, creole fish dish, **146–147**
fish, non-oily, **150–151**
fish, oily, **150**
fish sauce, devil of a, **153**
fish that swim through the door, **152–153**
french dressing, aunt bertha's american, **165**
gazpacho, **142**
iscas de porco, liver portuguese style, **158**
leftover-mashed-potato pancake, **163**
lulas, french-fried (squid), **149**

lulas recheadas (stuffed squid), **149**
macaroons, **169**
mayonnaise, blender, **164–165**
mayonnaise, processor, **165**
mayonnaise, super-rich, **164**
meringues, **168–169**
pão-de-ló, portuguese cafe cake, **172**
pâté, a simple country one, **143**
peas, interesting green, **159**
pie, cherry, **167**
pie crust, "southern pastry," **165–166**
pie crust, vinegar, **166**
pie, old-fashioned vinegar, **166–167**
piri-piri, hot pepper sauce, **155**
pollo al ajillo, spanish garlic chicken, **154**
potatoes, josé's non-lumpy mashed, **162**
poulet à l'ail, french garlic chicken, **155**
ratatouille provençale, **160**
ratatouille, george's, **161**
rice (nicerice), **164**
spaghetti sauce, emergency, **144**
spoonbread, **170**
tomatoes à *la provençale*, **161–162**
tomatoes, philadelphia fried, **161**
tortilla, josé's spanish, **163**
virginia fried apples, **169–170**
virginia ham, **157**
zucchini at its best, **162**